# TYLER FLORENCE
# FAMILY MEAL

## Also by Tyler Florence

*Stirring the Pot*

*Dinner at My Place*

*Tyler's Ultimate*

*Eat This Book*

*Tyler Florence's Real Kitchen*

# Tyler Florence
# Family Meal

*Bringing People Together Never Tasted Better*

Photographs by John Lee

RODALE®

## Notice

Mention of specific companies, organizations, or authorities in this book does
not imply endorsement by the author or publisher, nor does mention of specific
companies, organizations, or authorities imply that they endorse this book,
its author, or the publisher.

Internet addresses and telephone numbers given in this book were accurate
at the time it went to press.

Rodale books may be purchased for business or promotional use or for special sales.
For information, please write to:
Special Markets Department, Rodale Inc., 733 Third Avenue, New York, NY 10017.

Printed in the United States of America
Rodale Inc. makes every effort to use acid-free ♾, recycled paper ♻.

Book design by Ruba Abu-Nimah and Eleanor Rogers
Photographs by John Lee

**Library of Congress Cataloging-in-Publication Data**

Florence, Tyler.
    Tyler Florence family meal : bringing people together never tasted better / Tyler Florence ;
photographs by John Lee.
        p.    cm.
    Includes index.
    ISBN 978–1–60529–338–7   hardcover
    1. Cookbooks.   2. Families.   I. Title.   II. Title: Family meals.
   TX714.F636   2010
  641.5—dc22                                           2010035300

**Distributed to the trade by Macmillan**
2   4   6   8   10   9   7   5   3   1   hardcover

We inspire and enable people to improve their lives and the world around them.

Today, there is no single way to define a
family. In the simplest terms, it's the people
you spend a great deal of time with, care for
deeply, and trust with everything. A two-way,
never-ending street of giving and sharing with
green lights in both directions.

I'm dedicating this book to two people who have
lived incredible lives and who define our family,
two people that my wife, Tolan, and I can't thank
enough: her parents, Marge and Larry.

Tireless grandparents, best friends, drinking
companions, mediators, confidants, consiglieres,
and allies, they welcomed me into their family
six years ago and haven't looked back. Thank
you for sharing your lives with us, and thank you
for making each family meal special.

—T.F.

# Contents

# Introduction

When you hear the words *family meal*, no doubt you have immediate associations: a big pot of Sunday-night sauce with pasta; your grandmother's pot roast; a perfectly roasted chicken with pan gravy and mashed potatoes. Mention these words to a chef, though, and you evoke something else entirely. To those of you who've never worked in restaurants, family meal is the shared meal that is served to the entire restaurant staff before service starts each day. It is a restaurant ritual and a great source of pride among the up-and-coming cooks on the staff—not to mention a great way to air any dirty laundry, discuss the specials of the night, and (perhaps most important), keep theft down.

At my very first restaurant job, I often collaborated on family meal with a fellow dishwasher, a Polish émigré and former circus worker. The dinners we turned out were a hybrid of southern dishes and traditional Polish food: fried pork chops, for example, were turned into *golonka*, a classical Polish stew of pork knuckles cooked with caraway, cabbage, and whatever other vegetables we had in-house and mashed potatoes left over from the previous night were transformed into pierogis. Ultimately my coworker's demons got the best of him after a year-long tenure at the dish station, but I'll always remember him and how we tackled family meal together and how those meals helped me share a bit of who I was with the people in my work family through the food I made for them.

Since then there have been a *lot* of family meals under the bridge, and my family, both personal and professional, has expanded exponentially. The last fifteen years of my life are a collection of memories of kitchens, restaurants, and cooking with different chefs, in different countries and different cities.

From culinary and business schools at Johnson and Wales University in Charleston, South Carolina, to moving to New York City to work at Aureole with Charlie Palmer and his refined New American Cuisine, then on to Pino Luongo's Mad. 61 to learn classic Tuscan Italian; from line cook at the beautiful three-star River Café in Brooklyn (back in its heyday) to becoming the executive chef at Cibo by the time I was twenty-five—I've lived more life in the kitchen than outside it. Food defines me.

I've also had the opportunity to go around the world several times, mostly thanks to my family at Food Network. We've shot amazing programming in off-the-beaten-track locations that a restaurant-bound chef living in New York City would never have the chance to experience. I've been truffle hunting in Alba; and I've made prosciutto in Parma, pizza in Naples, fish and chips in London, bouillabaisse in Marseilles, dim sum in Hong Kong, mole in Oaxaca, jambalaya in New Orleans, fried chicken in Mississippi, and tapas in Barcelona. For a chef, it just doesn't get much better.

And in a way, everything I've done in my life has been a dress rehearsal for what's happening right now. Marin County, just north of San Francisco, is where I'm putting my roots down,

raising my family, and starting multiple business ventures. My wife, Tolan, and I have a lot on our plate with three restaurants; three kitchen stores; our new wines with the Michael Mondavi Family; Sprout, our organic baby-food company; our cutlery, cookware, spice, and sauce lines; and, of course, more television and books—all while raising three children. We call it the Florence Family Circus.

With all of these projects on the table and more in the pipeline, I've got to tell you, I've never been happier. I love my beautiful wife; my children, Miles, Hayden, and Dorothy; and all of the new members of my extended family, which grows with each new venture. It is this burgeoning extended family that brought me to the title of this book, *Family Meal*. With each project I take on, I gain a new group of people to work with who inspire me and who, as my associates, ultimately become part of my family. And to this day, whenever I find a new group of people ready to share their lives with me, my first instinct is to cook for them.

To me, the concept of *Family Meal* has transcended the restaurant kitchen to represent the way I interact with my friends, my family, my neighbors, my business partners, my

employees—and now, you. If you are a part of my life, I want to tell you about who I am through my food. Kitchens are all I know, food is all I think about, and when I cook for the people around me it shows you that I care—just as it does when you cook for the people in your own family, however it is configured.

For me, that's what it truly means to cook, whether I'm creating the menus for my restaurants or making pancakes in the kitchen with my middle child, Hayden. Over the past thirty-nine years, I've learned from and been influenced by an amazing group of colleagues, family members, and good friends; now it's my turn to share not just the recipes and techniques I've accumulated, but also what it means to cook a dish for someone else and put everything that's in your soul into that plate of food. I finally feel that I have learned enough that I can start teaching the next generation. I want to teach my children the emotion behind the act of providing. It's not the crispiness of my fried chicken that makes cooking my calling, or the creaminess of my potato puree that makes me feel good about myself. It's my ability to express my emotions and communicate my feelings through these dishes that is truly rewarding to me. And this kind of satisfaction doesn't come in a vacuum. It works just

like a telephone: There has to be a person on each end of the line for the circuit to be complete. My cooking and my food aren't worth a lick if there's nobody there for me to share them with.

This book is about the many families that are a part of my life right now. Some are new, some have been there for a while—and there will be new families to come. It's been an amazing journey, especially most recently here in the Bay Area, meeting the extraordinary people in the food world here—not just chefs, but the purveyors, farmers, and inspired home cooks all around me—and discovering the incredible bounty and impeccable food northern California has to offer. I look forward to cooking for all of them, and for you, in our restaurants in San Francisco, Mill Valley, and Napa. And I hope you'll use the recipes in *Family Meal* to connect with your family and friends and experience the same satisfaction that cooking with love has always given me.

So let's get the stoves cranked up and get cooking!

# Part 1

# Eating at Home:
## *Me and My Family*

Like many people of my generation and those that followed, I was a latchkey kid. My parents didn't leave me at home because they didn't care, nor because they didn't want to be with me. They had to work to give me a place to come home to and to keep that food in the fridge. In hindsight, who knows if I would ever even have found my calling if I hadn't been left alone to figure out how to put food on the table.

As a latchkey kid, I like to think that I have a good perspective, both as a chef and a father, on what it means to sit around a table and eat a daily meal with your family. Now, more than ever, families need to stick together. And it has been proven that there's a direct relationship between the well-being of your kids and how often you have regularly scheduled family meals. I'm as busy as anyone, but unless I'm out of town, I always find a way to sit down to dinner with my kids. When I prepare dinner for my family and we sit around the table, a sharing process goes on between us that transcends the food. My daughter, Dorothy, only knows a few words, but the smile on her face and the way she communicates at the table tell me loud and clear where she is at that moment, for that day, and in her young life in general. And I know that she can sense the same in me. That's what eating together is about: communicating with your loved ones and providing a constant support system that can be counted upon.

A couple of years ago, the National Center on Addiction at Columbia University released a decade-long study on this very subject, and what they found out is pretty staggering. The study indicated that teens who have dinner with their families fewer than three times per week are twice as likely to use tobacco or marijuana than teens who have frequent family dinners. Infrequent family dinners also greatly increase teen use of alcohol as well as add to the risk of depression and eating disorders. With younger kids, the effects are even more profound. So, together, we need to make an effort to make sure our families get some solid dinnertime.

It isn't always easy to get your kids (especially teens) to sit down for dinner without a TV front and center, a PlayStation at hand or an iPod hard-wired into their ears; but if you don't make the effort, I think the negatives are pretty apparent. And let's not forget that this concept goes beyond just kids and teens. Think about your partner. Or your parents. Or whoever. Go old-school and sit down with those that you care about and share a meal. Talk. Hug it out. Whatever it takes to keep that vital human connection alive and buzzing.

The recipes in this chapter are designed to make it as easy as possible to enjoy your own family meals, whether you're making a quick, kid-friendly meal of chicken strips or meat loaf, or pulling out the stops for a holiday or weekend meal. I'm no Dr. Phil and certainly am not qualified to walk you and your family through your problems, but I do know that if I can do one thing to encourage this process of keeping families healthy, it's helping you put good food on your table. At the very least, nobody can use a burnt casserole or an ill-conceived stew as an excuse for staying away. So, please enjoy these recipes that I love to serve the Florence family when it comes time to gather around the table.

Bon appétit.

# Brunch

# The Perfect Omelet

The making of the perfect omelet is a test chefs give young culinary talent as a gateway to employment, and it's a skill well worth perfecting for the home cook as well. This method produces one large omelet in the French style, bright yellow on the outside and soft and custard-like on the inside.

**Serves 4 to 6**

½ bunch asparagus, 8 to 10 spears, bottom 2 inches removed

1 cup sliced onions

Extra-virgin olive oil

Kosher salt and freshly ground black pepper

12 large eggs

½ cup heavy cream

2 tablespoons butter, melted and cooled

4 thin slices prosciutto, chopped

2 tablespoons fresh thyme leaves

4 to 6 slices sourdough bread, toasted

4 ounces round triple crème cheese

2 cups lightly packed arugula

1 lemon, halved

Fresh herbs, for garnish

**Preheat the oven to 375°F.** Place the asparagus on one end of a rimmed baking sheet and the onions on the other end. Drizzle the vegetables with olive oil; season with salt and pepper. Roast the vegetables for 15 minutes, then transfer the asparagus to a plate and return the onions to the oven. Roast the onions for another 20 minutes, or until soft and caramelized. Leave the oven on.

**In a bowl, whisk** together the eggs and cream. Beat in the melted butter and season with salt and pepper. Place a 10-inch nonstick pan on the stove over low heat and add the eggs. Use a rubber spatula to stir the eggs constantly as they cook to keep them from setting up. Continue to cook and stir the eggs until they have the consistency of soft custard.

**Quickly arrange the asparagus** and onions on top of the eggs and sprinkle with the prosciutto and thyme. Place in the oven and bake until the eggs are cooked and fluffy, about 10 minutes. While the omelet bakes, slice the cheese horizontally into 4 to 6 slices. Arrange the toast slices on a baking sheet and top each with a slice of cheese. Bake until the cheese is melted, 10 to 12 minutes.

**Gently slide the omelet** out of the pan onto a platter, rolling it over and around the filling as you go. Toss the arugula with a good squeeze of lemon juice and the 1 teaspoon olive oil, and mound on top of the toast slices. Drizzle the omelet with a touch of olive oil and sprinkle with herbs. Slice and serve with the toasts.

# Hayden's Special-Occasion Chocolate Chip Banana Pancakes

I make pancakes for my kids on a regular basis, but the chocolate chips and bananas are just for special breakfasts. One day while making these with my son Hayden, he added an extra egg to the batter I've been making for years, and I have to say that simple little addition made my old-standby recipe even better.

**Serves 3 to 4 (makes 6 to 8 pancakes)**

2 cups all-purpose flour

¼ cup sugar

3 teaspoons baking powder

2 teaspoons baking soda

3 large eggs

2 cups buttermilk

4 tablespoons (½ stick) unsalted butter, melted and cooled

½ cup chocolate chips

2 bananas, sliced ¼ inch thick

Confectioners' sugar

Maple syrup

**In a medium bowl,** whisk together the flour, sugar, baking powder, and baking soda. Combine the eggs and buttermilk in a large bowl and beat to incorporate. Add the flour mixture to the bowl and stir quickly just until combined; do not overmix. Stir in the melted butter and ¼ cup of the chocolate chips. Heat a griddle or large nonstick skillet over medium-low heat, and coat with nonstick cooking spray. Ladle the batter onto the griddle, using ¼ cup for each pancake.

**Cook until the pancakes** are covered with bubbles, 3 to 4 minutes; flip and cook until golden brown on both sides, another 2 to 3 minutes and a few chocolate chips. Sprinkle with confectioners' sugar and top with sliced bananas. Pass the maple syrup.

Every time I see our son Hayden push his kitchen stool over to where I'm cooking and say "Daddy, I help," it stops me cold, as if I'm looking back at my younger self repeating the same ritual with my own father. I love seeing the excitement in his eyes as I tie a kitchen towel around his waist, pour off a little of what I'm working on into a smaller bowl, and let him whisk it all over the counter. As we both proudly serve homemade pancakes to his mother, his older brother, and his baby sister—pancakes that he helped crack the eggs for, helped pour onto the griddle and serve—it's inspiring to see all of the wide-eyed enthusiasm of a three-year-old who really enjoys being around cooking. The way I see it, my kitchen is a sanctuary of nourishment and discovery, full of warm smells, flavors, and experiences that will hopefully bake into a memory that will last my children a lifetime. To see a smile on Hayden's face as we cook together is all I need to remind me that it's my turn to teach the next generation that we're all important, we're connected, and we care for each other— and in our house, we do it through food.

# Waffle French Toast with Warm Berry Compote

Looking at my old waffle iron one morning and realizing I hadn't made waffles in two years got me thinking of what else I could do with it. Combining the waffle iron—really just a skillet with ridges—with my French toast recipe was a lightbulb moment; now I can cook four pieces of French toast at a time instead of just two, which makes it easier for our family to eat breakfast together.

**Serves 4**

## Compote

5 cups seasonal mixed berries

½ cup granulated sugar

2 tablespoons honey

Grated zest of 1 lemon

## French Toast

3 large eggs

¼ cup whole milk

½ teaspoon pure vanilla extract

½ teaspoon ground cinnamon

8 thick slices brioche loaf or other egg bread

Confectioners' sugar, for dusting

**Make the compote:** Place the berries in a medium skillet over medium heat. Sprinkle them with the granulated sugar and honey and cook over medium heat for 10 minutes. As the berries cook they will begin to release their juices. Remove from the heat and stir in the lemon zest.

**Make the French toast:** Whisk together the eggs, milk, vanilla, and cinnamon until blended. Preheat your waffle iron and coat the grids with nonstick cooking spray. Gently dredge the bread slices in the egg batter and place on the waffle iron (how many you can cook at a time depends on the size of your waffle iron). Close the lid and cook until the French toast is crispy, 5 to 7 minutes. Sprinkle with the confectioners' sugar and serve hot with the warm berry compote.

# Classic Pecan Banana Bread

This banana bread recipe is something I like to serve to my family on Sunday mornings. I toast a slice and smear it with butter and honey. At the holidays I bake them in miniature loaf pans to give as gifts with a jar of honey from the bees in our backyard.

**Makes 1 loaf**

2 cups all-purpose flour

1½ teaspoons baking soda

½ teaspoon salt

4 overripe bananas

1 cup granulated sugar

¾ cup (1½ sticks) unsalted butter, melted and cooled

2 large eggs, at room temperature

1 teaspoon pure vanilla extract

½ cup pecans, finely chopped plus ¼ cup whole pecan halves

Confectioners' sugar, for dusting

**Preheat the oven to 350°F** and lightly grease a 9 by 5-inch loaf pan.

**In a large bowl,** combine the flour, baking soda, and salt; set aside. Mash 2 of the bananas with a fork in a small bowl, leaving them with a bit of texture. With an electric mixer, or by hand, beat the remaining bananas and the granulated sugar together like you mean it, for a good 3 minutes; you want a light and fluffy banana cream.

**Add the melted butter,** eggs, and vanilla; beat well and scrape down the sides of the bowl. Mix in the flour mixture just until incorporated; no need to overblend. Fold in the nuts and the mashed bananas with a rubber spatula. Pour the batter into the prepared loaf pan. Give the pan a good rap on the counter to release any air bubbles. Arrange the pecan halves decoratively on top of the batter.

**Bake for 1 hour** and 15 minutes, or until the loaf is golden brown and a toothpick inserted into the center comes out clean. Rotate the pan every 25 minutes to ensure even browning. Don't get nervous if the banana bread develops a crack down the center of the loaf; that's typical.

**Cool the bread in the pan** for 10 minutes or so, and then turn out onto a wire rack to cool completely before slicing. Toast the slices of banana bread, dust with confectioners' sugar, and serve.

# Potato and Chorizo Tortilla

I love a one-dish breakfast and this Spanish-inspired egg-and-potato combo is a great, hearty example. It works just as well at room temperature as it does hot out of the oven.

**Preheat the oven to 375°F.**

**Heat a 3-count of oil** in a 12-inch nonstick ovenproof skillet over medium-high heat. Add the chorizo and fry for 5 minutes, until some of the fat has been rendered. Add the potatoes and onions and cook, stirring, until the onions start to soften, about 5 minutes. Reduce the heat to low, cover the skillet, and cook until the potatoes are tender, about 15 minutes. Remove the cover, raise the heat to high, and cook until the potatoes are brown and crispy all over, another 5 to 10 minutes.

**Break the eggs into** a large bowl. Add the milk, season with salt and pepper, and whisk until frothy. Pour the egg mixture into the pan, shaking it to distribute the eggs evenly. Slide the pan into the oven and cook until the tortilla is puffy and set, 12 to 15 minutes. Turn the tortilla out onto a cutting board and let it cool to room temperature.

**To serve, toss the** greens with a tablespoon of oil and the lemon juice; season with salt and pepper. Cut the tortilla into thin wedges, and serve topped with some of the greens.

### Serves 6 to 8

Extra-virgin olive oil

4 dried Spanish chorizo sausages, sliced ¼ inch thick

3 medium Yukon Gold potatoes, cut into ¼-inch-thick rounds

1 medium onion, chopped

8 large eggs

½ cup whole milk

Kosher salt and freshly ground black pepper

1 cup mixed baby greens or arugula

Juice of ½ lemon

# Big Breakfast Fry-Up

This fry-up starts with browned button mushrooms and caramelized tomatoes cooked in the renderings of crisp bacon or pancetta, and it all goes on top of a skilletful of sunnyside-up eggs. Serve it rustic style, right from the skillet, with a big pile of freshly toasted country bread. It's a great family breakfast.

**Serves 4 to 6**

6 to 8 strips smoked bacon slices or 4 (¼-inch-thick) slices pancetta, cut in 2-inch pieces

1 cup halved button mushrooms

1 cup grape or cherry tomatoes, halved

Kosher salt and freshly ground black pepper

Extra-virgin olive oil

6 to 8 large eggs

Fresh thyme leaves

A handful of baby arugula

6 to 8 slices Italian country loaf, toasted

**In a large skillet,** cook the bacon over medium heat until crispy, 5 to 6 minutes. Transfer the bacon to a paper-towel-lined plate to drain, leaving the fat in the skillet. Add the mushrooms and tomatoes to the pan and sauté over medium-high heat for 3 to 5 minutes, until the mushrooms are lightly browned and the tomatoes are caramelized. Sprinkle with salt and pepper. Remove the mixture to a plate and set aside.

**Reduce the heat to low,** and add 1 to 2 teaspoons olive oil to the skillet if needed. Carefully crack the eggs into the skillet. Cook the eggs sunnyside up, or until the whites are set but the yolks are still runny.

**Distribute the bacon,** mushrooms, and tomatoes evenly around the pan, and sprinkle with salt, pepper, thyme, arugula, and a drizzle of olive oil. Serve right from the pan, with the toasted bread.

# Huevos Rancheros

*with* SALSA ROJA

I've driven through most of Mexico, and huevos rancheros is hands down that country's most popular breakfast. It means "eggs country style" in Spanish, and the dish was traditionally served to farm and ranch hands for their midmorning meals. I've slightly updated this dish with a salsa roja ("red sauce") that uses both fresh and dried chiles, and I've added Spanish chorizo to the refried beans to make the dish a bit more substantial and even more delicious.

**To make the salsa roja:** Tear the ancho, anaheim, and chipotle chiles into large pieces and toast them in a dry skillet over medium heat until they change color a bit, about 2 minutes. Add the cumin, coriander, and oregano and continue to toast for 2 to 3 minutes, until everything is fragrant. Remove from the heat and carefully add about 1 cup hot water to the skillet to just cover the chiles. Set aside to soak for 20 minutes.

**Preheat the broiler.** Spread the tomatoes, onion, jalapeño, and garlic cloves onto a rimmed baking sheet. Drizzle with plenty of olive oil and season well with salt and pepper. Place under the broiler for 5 to 6 minutes until everything is nicely charred—you want lots of deep rich color, so don't be afraid if some of the edges get pretty black. Transfer the vegetables to a blender and puree. Add the chiles and their soaking liquid and continue to puree until smooth (you may need to do this in two batches). Return the sauce to the skillet, season with salt and pepper, and stir in the lime juice.

*(continued on page 23)*

**Serves 4**

*Salsa Roja*

1 dried ancho chile, stemmed and seeded

1 dried Anaheim chile, stemmed and seeded

1 dried chipotle chile, stemmed and seeded

2 tablespoons ground cumin

1 tablespoon ground coriander

1 tablespoon dried oregano

8 plum tomatoes, quartered

1 medium Spanish onion, sliced

1 jalapeño chile, split lengthwise

4 garlic cloves

Extra-virgin olive oil

Kosher salt and freshly ground black pepper

2 tablespoons fresh lime juice

Peanut or vegetable oil, for frying

4 medium corn tortillas

1 tablespoon extra-virgin olive oil

4 large eggs

Chorizo Refried Beans (page 23)

¼ cup chopped fresh cilantro leaves

1 cup crumbled queso fresco

4 lime wedges

2 radishes, sliced

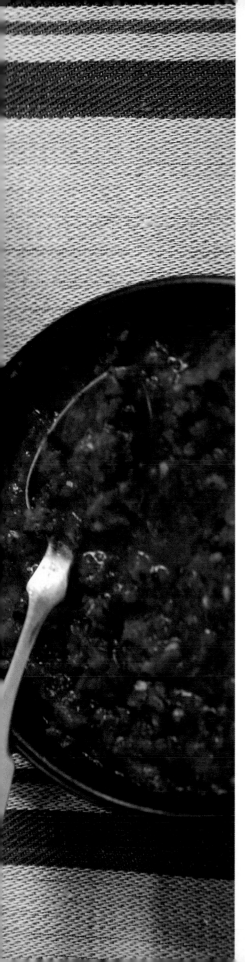

Heat 1 inch of peanut oil in a deep, straight-sided skillet to 375°F. One at a time, carefully lower the tortillas into the hot oil and fry for 20 seconds on each side. Drain briefly on paper towels, then dip the still-hot tortillas into the salsa roja, turning to evenly coat both sides. Place each on a serving plate.

Heat a 10-inch cast iron skillet over medium high heat for 2 minutes. Add the 1 tablespoon olive oil and swirl it around, then carefully crack the eggs into the pan, leaving some space between them. Cook the eggs for 4 minutes, or until the white is cooked and the yolk has just begun to set around the edges, but is still runny.

Spread a large dollop of the chorizo refried beans in the center of each tortilla, then top with an egg. Sprinkle with cilantro, queso fresco, and radish slices, and serve with a lime wedge.

# Chorizo Refried Beans

**Makes 4 cups**

4 links dried Spanish chorizo sausages, roughly chopped

¼ cup extra-virgin olive oil

¼ white onion, finely diced

2 garlic cloves, chopped

2 (15.5-ounce) cans red kidney beans, drained and rinsed

3 cups low-sodium chicken broth

Kosher salt and freshly ground black pepper

Place the chorizo in a food processor and pulse to make rough crumbs. Heat the oil in a heavy-bottomed pot over medium heat. Add the chorizo and cook to render some of the fat and infuse the oil, about 10 minutes. Use a slotted spoon to remove about ¼ cup of the fried crumbles and set aside.

Add the onion and garlic to the pot with the chorizo, raise the heat to medium-high, and cook until the vegetables are slightly soft and translucent, about 5 minutes. Add the beans and broth and simmer for 10 minutes to allow the flavors to come together. Season with salt and pepper. Use a potato masher to mash the beans into a coarse puree, or puree in a food processor if you prefer a smoother texture. Serve sprinkled with the reserved chorizo crumbles.

# Gallina de Madre

## "MOTHER HEN" TOAST

I had this dish on a trip to Barcelona many years ago and it remains one of my favorites. It is a new twist on ham and eggs for breakfast, and when I have friends and family staying with us, I like to load up an entire baking sheet.

**Make the Manchego** béchamel sauce: Melt the butter in a saucepan over medium heat. Add the flour and cook, whisking constantly, for 2 to 3 minutes; do not allow the mixture to take on any color. Gradually whisk in the milk and continue to cook, whisking, until the mixture thickens and comes to a boil. Add the cheese and stir for another minute until it is completely melted. Stir in the horseradish and nutmeg, season with salt and pepper, and keep warm while you prepare the eggs.

**Preheat the oven to 400°F.**
Arrange the bread on a rimmed baking sheet and drizzle with olive oil. Season with salt and pepper. Toast in the oven until barely golden, about 10 minutes.

**Arrange 1 slice of** ham on each toast slice, forming it into a nest shape. Carefully break an egg into each nest and sprinkle with salt and pepper. Return the baking sheet to the oven and bake until the eggs are set but the yolks are still slightly runny, about 10 minutes.

**While the eggs bake,** heat ½ inch of olive oil in a small skillet over medium-high heat. Add the sage leaves and fry until crisp and dark, about 2 minutes. Drain on paper towels.

**Transfer an egg toast** to each plate and spoon some of the Manchego béchamel over each. Garnish with a fried sage leaf.

**Serves 6**

### Manchego Béchamel

2 tablespoons (¼ stick) unsalted butter

1½ heaping tablespoons all-purpose flour

1 cup whole milk

1 cup grated Manchego cheese

1½ teaspoons prepared horseradish

Pinch grated nutmeg

Kosher salt and freshly ground black pepper

---

6 thick slices Italian or French country bread

Extra-virgin olive oil

Kosher salt and freshly ground black pepper

8 paper-thin slices Serrano ham

6 eggs

6 fresh sage leaves

# Simple Dinners

# Asparagus Risotto

## with BLACK TRUFFLE AND POACHED EGG

This is pure spring, combining of some of my favorite ingredients in the world: asparagus, black truffle, and a perfectly soft poached egg.

**Serves 6**

Kosher salt

1 bunch asparagus, 14 to 16 spears, bottom 2 inches removed

2 tablespoons extra-virgin olive oil

Freshly ground black pepper

3 tablespoons unsalted butter

½ yellow onion, finely diced

1 garlic clove, minced

6½ cups low-sodium chicken or vegetable broth

2 cups Arborio rice

1 cup dry white wine

½ cup shredded Parmesan cheese

1 tablespoon white vinegar

6 eggs

1 small fresh black truffle or 2 tablespoons black truffle oil (optional)

**Preheat the oven to 400°F.**

**Fill a large bowl** with ice water and bring a large skillet of salted water to a boil over high heat. Add half of the asparagus to the skillet and blanch for 1 minute, or until it is bright green. Immediately plunge the asparagus into the ice water to stop the cooking process. Transfer the blanched asparagus to a blender and puree for 1 to 2 minutes, or until smooth. Toss the remaining asparagus with the olive oil on a rimmed baking sheet and season with salt and pepper. Roast the asparagus for 10 to 12 minutes, or until the asparagus is tender when pierced with a fork.

**Melt the butter in** a heavy-bottomed pot over medium heat. Add the onions and garlic and cook slowly until the onions are translucent, about 10 minutes. In a separate pot, bring the broth to a boil. Once the onions are translucent, add the rice to the onions, and cook for 2 or 3 minutes. Add the wine and stir until the wine has been completely absorbed by the rice. Begin to add the hot broth to the rice a ladleful at a time, making sure the previous addition of broth has been totally absorbed by the rice before adding more. Cook, stirring frequently, until all the broth has been absorbed and the rice is creamy but with a slight bite to it. Stir in the cheese and season with salt and pepper. Set aside and keep warm.

**Bring a saucepan of** water to a gentle rolling boil. Add the vinegar and a pinch of salt. Crack the eggs into a saucer one at a time and gently slide them into the water. Poach for 2 minutes, or until the whites are set but the yolks are still runny. Carefully drain the eggs on a paper towel.

**To serve, stir the** asparagus puree into the risotto and spoon into shallow bowls. Gently arrange a poached egg and some roasted asparagus on top of each portion. Shave a bit of black truffle over the top or drizzle with a bit of truffle oil, if desired.

# Angel Hair Pasta

## with CHILE, LEMON, *and* ARUGULA

This is my go-to recipe for nights when the pantry and fridge are looking a bit bare. It's made from things we always have on hand in our house: boxes of pasta, a big bowl of lemons, a few chunks of fresh Parmesan. Always try to buy a few simple pantry items like these in larger quantities so you can whip up a pasta like this at a moment's notice.

**Serves 4 to 6**

2 cups panko bread crumbs

8 tablespoons extra-virgin olive oil

Kosher salt and freshly ground black pepper

3 garlic cloves, slivered

¼ teaspoon dried red pepper flakes

Grated zest of 1 lemon

1 pound angel hair pasta

2 cups lightly packed baby or wild arugula

**In a skillet, combine** the panko with 2 tablespoons of the oil and toss to combine. Toast over medium heat, stirring, until the bread crumbs are golden brown, about 10 minutes. Season with salt and pepper, then transfer to a small bowl.

**In the same skillet,** heat the remaining 6 tablespoons of olive oil over medium heat. Add the garlic and red pepper flakes and cook for 10 to 12 minutes to infuse the oil and gently cook the garlic. Season with salt and pepper. Stir in the lemon zest and remove from the heat.

**Bring a large pot** of well-salted water to a boil. Add the pasta and cook for 3 to 4 minutes, or until al dente. Drain the pasta well, and transfer to a large bowl. Immediately add the arugula, the infused oil with the garlic, and the bread crumbs. Use tongs to gently toss everything together. Mound the pasta on a large platter and serve.

# Grilled Pizza with Braised Rainbow Chard

## CHILI OIL, *and* MOZZARELLA

**Pizza dough is a lot easier to make than people think, and this recipe of mine is pretty tried and true. Use this recipe as a template for topping your pizza with whatever is fresh and in season.**

**Combine the oil, smoked** paprika, and chili powder in a small saucepan. Bring to a simmer over low heat, whisking to prevent the spices from settling to the bottom and burning. Remove from the heat and let cool. (The chili oil can be stored in an airtight container in the refrigerator for up to 1 month.)

**Place a large skillet** over high heat and add a 2-count of extra-virgin olive oil. Once the oil starts to shimmer, add the chopped chard, salt, and pepper to taste. Sauté until the chard has wilted but still has a slight bit of crunch. Remove from the heat and add the lemon zest. Set aside.

**Set a gas grill** to high heat. If using a charcoal grill, pile the briquettes higher on one side and lower on the other for a hot side and a medium side. Oil the grill

grates with olive oil. Roll out the pizza dough to a ¼-inch thickness and rub surface with oil. Place the dough directly on the hottest part of the grill. Grill the dough until slightly charred, then turn and grill the second side until cooked.

**Transfer the crust to** a cutting board and distribute the chard evenly over the crust. Arrange the cheese on top. Return the pizza to the grill, reducing the heat to medium or placing it over the less hot part of the fire. Cover the grill and cook the pizza until the cheese has begun to melt. Transfer to a cutting board.

**In a bowl, toss the greens** with the lemon juice and 1 tablespoon of olive oil. Scatter the greens on top of the pizza and drizzle with the chili oil. Garnish with edible flowers, if desired.

**Serves 8 to 10**

### *Smoked Paprika Chili Oil*

1 cup extra-virgin olive oil

2 teaspoons smoked paprika (pimentón)

1 teaspoon chili powder

---

Extra-virgin olive oil

2 bunches rainbow chard, tough stems removed, chopped

1 teaspoon kosher salt

Freshly ground black pepper

Grated zest and juice of 1 lemon

Pizza Dough for the Grill (page 35)

3 balls Hand-Pulled Mozzarella (page 39) or fresh store-bought mozzarella, 8 to 10 ounces total, thickly sliced

2 cups wild greens, such as arugula, dandelion, or mesclun

Edible flowers (optional)

# Pizza Dough for the Grill

One of the best recipes any parent can master is making pizza dough. Most kids love pizza, and being able to give them a totally home-made, wholesome version makes you feel better about letting them eat their fill. Think of all the pizza parties in your future.

**In the bowl of** a standing electric mixer fitted with a dough hook, or in a mixing bowl, combine the yeast, sugar, and warm water and stir gently to dissolve. Let the mixture stand until the yeast comes alive and starts to foam, 5 to 10 minutes.

**If you're using a** mixer, turn the mixer on low and add the salt and olive oil. Add the flour, a little at a time, mixing at the lowest speed until the flour has been completely incorporated. When the dough starts to come together, increase the speed to medium and let it go until the dough gathers into a ball. This should take about 5 minutes. Stop the machine periodically to scrape the dough off the hook. Get a feel for the dough as you're making it by squeezing a small amount together between your thumb and fingers. If it's crumbly, add more water, if it's sticky, add more flour, 1 tablespoon at a time. Turn the dough out onto a lightly floured surface and fold it over itself a few times, kneading until it's smooth and elastic.

**If you're making the** dough by hand, stir in the salt and the olive oil. Then begin stirring in the flour. When the mixture becomes too stiff to stir with a wooden spoon, knead the rest of the flour in by hand, adding just enough to make a dough that is soft but not too sticky. As you work, squeeze a small amount of dough together between your thumb and fingers. If it's crumbly, add more water; if it's sticky, add more flour, 1 tablespoon at a time. Knead until smooth and elastic, about 5 minutes.

**Form the dough into** a ball and put it into a lightly oiled bowl, turning it over to coat the dough entirely with the oil. Cover with plastic wrap or a damp towel and let it rise in a warm spot (for example, over a gas pilot light) until doubled in size, about 1 hour.

**Makes enough for 1 large oval pizza or 2 smaller pizzas**

1 package active dry yeast

1 teaspoon sugar

1 cup warm (100°F to 110°F) water

1 tablespoon kosher salt

2 tablespoons extra-virgin olive oil

3 cups unbleached all-purpose flour, plus more for dusting

# Grilled Pizza with Parmesan Béchamel,

## EGGS, *and* SAUTÉED MUSHROOMS

We make this with beautiful fresh eggs we get from our friends Dennis and Sandy Dierks' farm—notice how perfectly yellow the yolks are—but feel free to adapt it to what you bring home from the farmer's market.

**Make the Parmesan béchamel** sauce: Melt the butter in a saucepan over medium heat. Add the flour and stir constantly for a few minutes to cook the flour; do not allow it to take on any color. Gradually pour in the milk as you stir and whisk out any lumps. Continue to stir until the mixture reaches a boil and thickens, then add the Parmesan cheese and nutmeg. Season with salt and pepper; set aside and keep warm.

**Set a skillet over** high heat and add the butter. When the butter melts, add the shallots and sauté for 20 seconds, then add the mushrooms. Sauté until the moisture has evaporated and the mushrooms have developed a nice golden color, about 5 minutes; season with salt and pepper.

**Set a gas grill** to high heat. If using a charcoal grill, pile the briquettes higher on one side and lower on the other for a hot side and a medium side. Oil the grill grates with olive oil. Roll out the pizza dough to a ¼-inch thickness and place directly on the grill over the hottest part of the flame. Grill on both sides until slightly charred, then transfer to a cutting board. While the crust cooks, grill the onions until soft and slightly charred, about 5 minutes.

**Spoon the béchamel onto** the pizza crust and spread evenly. Dot with the mushrooms and arrange the spring onions on top. Return the pizza to the grill, reducing the heat to medium or placing it over the less hot part of the fire, and gently crack the eggs on top. Cover the grill and cook until the eggs have just set, 5 to 7 minutes. Remove from the heat and sprinkle with the Parmesan and flowers, if using.

*Parmesan Béchamel*

4 tablespoons (½ stick) unsalted butter

3 heaping tablespoons all-purpose flour

1½ to 2 cups whole milk

½ cup grated Parmesan cheese

¼ teaspoon grated nutmeg

Kosher salt and freshly ground black pepper

---

2 tablespoons unsalted butter

1 shallot, minced

½ pound wild mushrooms, such as hedgehog, hen-of-the-woods, chanterelle, or morel mushrooms, torn into 2-inch pieces

Kosher salt and freshly ground black pepper

Pizza Dough for the Grill (page 35)

1 bunch spring onions, roots trimmed, or 1 red onion, thickly sliced

4 large fresh eggs

Freshly grated Parmesan cheese

Edible flowers (optional)

# Hand-Pulled Mozzarella

Fresh mozzarella is fun and easy to make. Just start with fresh curd, which can be purchased online at goldenagecheese.com. You may also be able to buy it locally from a store that makes its own fresh mozzarella.

To stretch and form the balls, fill a large bowl with very hot water; it should feel like a hot bath, approximately 120°F. Add a generous amount of salt. You want it to be about as salty as ocean water (in fact, mozzarella used to be made with fresh seawater). Place a second large bowl filled with ice water nearby. Drop 12 ounces of fresh mozzarella curd into the hot salted water and when it softens, fold and pull it like taffy. Don't overwork the curd, as this will make your finished cheese rubbery. If the water cools too much and the curd begins to harden, simply pour off the water and add more hot water. When soft and smooth, divide the curds into 4 portions and form each into a ball. Plunge the mozzarella balls into the ice water to cool. Store in the refrigerator, covered in cold salted water, for up to 1 week.

# Chicken Paillard

*with* SALAD GREENS *and* CREAMY PARMESAN DRESSING

I make this for dinner all the time. It's simple, easy to put together, and on the lighter side—perfect for a night when you want something delicious that's not too heavy. Pound the chicken between sheets of plastic wrap to keep your cutting board clean, and try to use organic, free-range chicken whenever you can.

**Place the chicken breasts** between two pieces of plastic wrap and gently pound with a mallet or rolling pin to a uniform ½-inch thickness. Prepare a breading station, placing the flour, seasoned with salt and pepper, in one shallow bowl; the eggs in another; and the panko (also seasoned liberally with salt and pepper—you should be able to see the seasonings) in a third. Coat the breasts first in the flour, then in the egg, and finally in the panko, shaking off the excess after each step. Place the breaded breasts on a plate and refrigerate for 10 minutes or so to dry the crust; this will ensure there is less moisture in the coating and less chance it will crumble when you cook the breasts.

**In a large skillet,** heat 2 inches of olive oil to 350ºF. Add the breasts and fry for 5 to 7 minutes per side, or until golden brown. Transfer the breasts to a paper-towel-lined plate to drain, and season with salt and pepper.

**Make the dressing: Combine** the anchovies, egg yolks, garlic, and lemon juice in a blender and process for 30 seconds, or until the mixture is smooth. With the blender running, slowing add the olive oil and blend until thick and creamy. Add a tablespoon or so of water if the dressing is too thick. Stir in the Parmesan and a couple of grinds of black pepper. (Refrigerate the dressing if you will not be using it right away.) Combine the salad greens, tomatoes, and bocconcini in a large mixing bowl. Add the dressing and toss well.

**To serve, place each** warm, crispy chicken paillard on a plate and top with half the salad. Serve with a wedge of lemon and a drizzle of olive oil.

## Serves 2

2 boneless, skinless chicken breast halves, about 8 ounces each

½ cup all-purpose flour

Kosher salt and freshly ground black pepper

2 eggs, lightly beaten

1 cup panko bread crumbs

Vegetable or peanut oil, for frying

### Dressing

4 anchovy fillets

2 egg yolks

1 garlic clove, peeled and smashed

Juice of 2 lemons

½ cup extra-virgin olive oil

¼ cup freshly grated Parmesan cheese

Freshly ground black pepper

### Salad

1 (3-ounce) bag mixed salad greens or arugula

1 pint organic grape tomatoes, halved

½ pound bocconcini (fresh mozzarella balls), halved

Fresh lemon wedges

Extra-virgin olive oil, for drizzling

# Tolan's Glazed Turkey Meat Loaf

My wife's family is from Wyoming, so she comes from a long line of meat-and-potatoes lovers. These days we're eating less red meat, so her family recipe got a makeover with ground turkey. The key to this recipe is the glaze, which adds enough flavor to make you forget you're eating turkey.

**Preheat the oven to 350°F.** Line a rimmed baking sheet with parchment paper. Combine the bread and milk in a small bowl and set aside for several minutes.

**In a medium skillet,** sauté the onions, diced bacon, and garlic over medium heat for 10 minutes, or until the onions are translucent; scrape the mixture into a large mixing bowl and allow to cool for 5 minutes or so.

**Add the ground turkey,** milk-soaked bread (discard any remaining milk), egg, ketchup, Worcestershire, and salt to the bowl with the onions and mix well. Divide the mixture in half and form each portion into an oblong mound on the prepared baking sheet. Top with the bacon strips.

**Make the glaze:** In a small saucepan, combine the ketchup, mustard, and brown sugar and bring to a boil, stirring frequently. Use a pastry brush to paint a thick layer of the glaze onto each bacon-wrapped meat loaf.

**Bake until the internal** temperature reaches 160°F, or about 1 hour. Let the meat loaves rest for at least 20 minutes before slicing and serving.

## Serves 8

2 slices soft white bread, torn into pieces

2 cups whole milk

1 large yellow onion, diced

1 cup diced thick-cut bacon, plus 6 to 8 strips

2 garlic cloves, minced

2 pounds ground turkey breast

1 large egg

3 tablespoons ketchup

2 tablespoons Worcestershire sauce

2 tablespoons salt

## Glaze

1 cup ketchup

½ cup Dijon mustard

1 cup lightly packed light brown sugar

# Barbecued Chicken and Pineapple Skewers

My kids love barbecue sauce, period, and anything on skewers is just more fun, so this is a win-win. It's one of our go-to family meals.

**In a saucepan, combine** the ketchup, soy sauce, honey, mustard, brown sugar, garlic, and lemon juice and stir to blend. Bring to a simmer over medium heat and cook gently until thickened, about 10 minutes. Set aside.

**Prepare a medium fire** in a charcoal grill, preheat your gas grill to medium, or heat a ridged grill pan on the stovetop over medium-high heat. With a sharp knife, slice off the pineapple rind. Cut the pineapple lengthwise into 3 long wedges, cut off and discard the core, and cut the pineapple into 1½-inch chunks. Cut each chicken thigh into 2 pieces.

**Thread the chicken** and pineapple pieces onto the skewers, alternating the chicken and pineapple. Brush with olive oil and season with salt and pepper. Remove the garlic cloves from the sauce and discard. Reserve about half of the sauce for serving, then brush the skewers with the remaining sauce.

**Grill the skewers,** turning often and basting occasionally with barbecue sauce, until cooked through, 10 to 15 minutes. Serve with the reserved sauce on the side for dipping.

## Serves 4 to 6

1 cup ketchup

¼ cup low-sodium soy sauce

¼ cup honey

1 tablespoon yellow mustard

¼ cup packed light brown sugar

2 garlic cloves, peeled and smashed with the side of a chef's knife

Juice of 1 lemon

½ fresh pineapple

6 large boneless, skinless chicken thighs

Kosher salt and freshly ground black pepper

12 wooden skewers, soaked in water for 30 minutes

Olive oil, for brushing

# Hayden's Favorite Breaded Chicken Strips

Kids love chicken fingers—there is no way around it. Rather than fight that battle, I make them as healthy as possible, using organic chicken whenever possible and baking them in the oven rather than frying them. My wife, Tolan, always keeps a bag of organic sweet potato fries in the freezer for the perfect quick kid-friendly meal when we're pressed for time.

**Serves 4**

8 slices sourdough or other white bread (about 8 ounces)

3 tablespoons grated Parmesan cheese

2 tablespoons minced fresh flat-leaf parsley

Kosher salt and freshly ground black pepper

About 1 cup all-purpose flour

2 large eggs, beaten

3 boneless, skinless chicken breast halves, about 8 ounces each

**Preheat the oven to 375°F.** Line a baking sheet with parchment paper.

**Tear the bread into** pieces, spread on a microwaveable plate, and microwave on high for 1 minute to dry out the bread. Pulse the dried bread in a food processor with the Parmesan, parsley, ¾ teaspoon salt, and ¼ teaspoon pepper to make fine crumbs.

**Put the flour, eggs,** and bread-crumb mixture in 3 separate shallow dishes.

**With the side of** a chef's knife or the smooth side of a meat pounder, pound each breast to a ½-inch thickness between 2 sheets of plastic wrap. Pat the chicken dry, cut lengthwise into 1-inch-wide strips, and season all over with salt and pepper. Dip each strip into the flour and shake off the excess. Next, run the strips through the egg to coat them lightly, allowing the excess to drip back into the bowl. Finally, lay the strips in the bread crumbs and press them into the breading to coat evenly on all sides.

**Arrange the breaded chicken** strips on the prepared baking sheet and bake until the chicken is cooked through and the bread crumbs are golden brown, 25 to 30 minutes.

# California Mussel Chowder

## with FRESH MEXICAN CHORIZO

I've never tasted finer oysters and clams or more succulent black mussels than those that come from the waters north of San Francisco. Meaty mussels, ever so lightly stewed with cream and rich pork fat, is a mind-blowing combination.

**In a large stockpot,** cook the bacon and chorizo over medium heat until the fat renders and the bacon and chorizo are slightly crispy, about 15 minutes. Add the potatoes, onions, celery, garlic, and thyme and cook for about 10 minutes, stirring occasionally, until the vegetables are tender. Add the wine and cook until the liquid is reduced by half, 3 to 5 minutes. Stir in the flour, making sure to coat all of the vegetables evenly, then add the broth and half-and-half. Raise the heat to medium-high and bring the soup to a simmer, stirring constantly, then reduce the heat to low, cover the pot, and simmer for 30 minutes.

**While the soup simmers,** preheat the oven to 375°F. Combine the panko, rosemary, parsley, and thyme in a food processor and chop fine. Spread out on a rimmed baking sheet, season with the salt, and drizzle with the oil. Bake for 5 to 7 minutes or until crispy and lightly golden. Set aside.

**Add the mussels to** the simmering soup, cover the pot again, and cook for 5 to 10 minutes, or until all the mussels have opened (discard any that do not open). Season to taste with salt and pepper and serve in shallow soup bowls with a generous sprinkling of the seasoned bread crumbs.

### Serve 6 to 8

1 cup diced bacon

1 pound fresh Mexican chorizo, casings removed

3 Yukon Gold potatoes, peeled and cubed

1 large yellow onion, diced

4 celery stalks, diced

3 garlic cloves, peeled and smashed with the side of a chef's knife

8 fresh thyme sprigs

½ cup dry white wine

3 tablespoons all-purpose flour

1 quart low-sodium chicken broth

3 cups half-and-half

2 cups panko bread crumbs

2 teaspoons chopped fresh rosemary

2 tablespoons chopped fresh flat-leaf parsley

1 tablespoon chopped fresh thyme leaves

2 teaspoons kosher salt

1 tablespoon extra-virgin olive oil

3 pounds mussels, preferably cultivated, scrubbed

Kosher salt and freshly ground black pepper

# Sole Almondine

This is a great entry-level way to prepare fish for those who don't consider themselves fish lovers. The flavors are mild, bright, and not at all aggressive. You can substitute thin fillets of any white fish, such as flounder or turbot.

**Serves 4 to 6**

½ cup coarsely chopped almonds

Kosher salt

Extra-virgin olive oil

Freshly ground black pepper

1 cup all-purpose flour

1 egg, lightly beaten

4 sole fillets, about 6 ounces each

2 tablespoons unsalted butter

2 small shallots, finely chopped

½ cup dry white wine

Juice of 1 lemon

¼ cup chopped fresh flat-leaf parsley

Lemon Smashed Yukon Potatoes
(page 85)

**In a large nonstick** skillet, toast the almonds over medium heat for 5 to 7 minutes, or until golden brown. Season with a sprinkle of salt, then transfer to a small bowl and set aside.

**Return the pan to** medium heat and add a 2-count of oil. Place the flour in a shallow dish and season liberally with salt and pepper. Place the eggs in another shallow dish. Working with 2 fillets at a time, dredge the fish in the seasoned flour, coating both sides evenly. Shake gently to remove the excess flour, then dip in the beaten eggs, allowing some of the excess egg to drip back into the dish. Dredge again in the flour. Place the fillets directly into the hot pan and cook

2 to 3 minutes, then carefully turn the fillets over and add 1 tablespoon of the butter to the pan. Spoon the melted butter over the fillets as they cook on the second side, about 30 seconds; this ensures that the fish remains moist. Transfer the fillets to a platter and keep warm while you repeat with the remaining fillets and butter.

**Add the shallots to** the same pan and cook over medium heat until transluscent, about 3 minutes. Add the white wine and stir to loosen the bits from the bottom of the pan, then add the lemon juice and parsley. Serve the fillets on a bed of smashed potatoes with the sauce spooned on top and sprinkled with the toasted almonds.

# Beef Bourguignon

I haven't done much to this earthy classic—why tamper with perfection? Serve it in deep bowls over buttered noodles with parsley for a soul-satisfying winter meal.

**Serves 8 to 10**

Extra-virgin olive oil

4 bacon slices

4 pounds beef chuck or round, cut into 2-inch cubes

Kosher salt and freshly ground black pepper

½ cup all-purpose flour

¼ cup Cognac

1 bottle dry red wine, such as Burgundy

2 cups low-sodium beef broth

2 tablespoons tomato paste

Bouquet garni (1 fresh rosemary sprig, 8 fresh thyme sprigs, and 2 bay leaves, tied together with kitchen twine or wrapped in cheesecloth)

4 garlic cloves, chopped

2 cups pearl onions, fresh or frozen, blanched and peeled

1 pound white mushrooms, stems trimmed

Pinch of sugar

2 tablespoons unsalted butter

Chopped fresh flat-leaf parsley, for garnish

**Place a large, heavy** pot over medium heat and drizzle in a 1-count of oil. Fry the bacon until crisp, about 5 minutes, then remove it to paper towels to drain, leaving the rendered fat in the pan. When cool, crumble the bacon and set aside.

**Working in batches, add** the beef to the pot and brown well on all sides over high heat, about 10 minutes per batch. Season each batch with a generous amount of salt and pepper and transfer to a plate while you brown the remaining beef cubes.

**Return all the beef** cubes to the pot and sprinkle with the flour, stirring to make sure the pieces are well coated. Pour in the Cognac and stir to scrape up the flavorful bits from the bottom of the pan. Cook over high heat until the Cognac has evaporated, about 10 minutes. Pour in the red wine and beef broth; then add the tomato paste and bouquet garni. Stir everything together and bring the liquid to a simmer. Cook uncovered until the liquid has thickened a bit, about 15 minutes, then cover the pot, reduce the heat to low, and simmer for 1 hour.

**Add the garlic, pearl** onions, and mushrooms to the pot along with the sugar (to balance out the acid from the red wine). Season with salt and pepper. Turn the heat up slightly and simmer 30 to 45 minutes longer, until the vegetables and meat are tender. Discard the bouquet garni, then stir in the butter to give the sauce a rich flavor and beautiful shine. Sprinkle with chopped parsley and the reserved bacon before serving.

# Slow-Roasted Veal Shoulder

DUSTED *with* DRIED PORCINI MUSHROOMS

Veal shoulder is a great value compared to more popular cuts like chops and loin roasts and is woefully underused in my opinion. When cooked low and slow, it delivers amazing flavor without much effort. Dried porcini mushrooms add a welcome earthy note.

**Serves 8 to 10**

4 cups dried porcini mushrooms

3 tablespoons kosher salt

2 tablespoons onion powder

2 tablespoons garlic powder

2 tablespoons freshly ground black pepper

5- to 6-pound boneless veal shoulder

Extra-virgin olive oil

**Preheat the oven to 300°F.**

**Place the porcinis in** a clean coffee mill or spice grinder and grind to a fine powder. Transfer to a small bowl and stir in the salt, onion powder, garlic powder, and pepper.

**Place the veal on** a parchment-lined baking sheet and rub with a bit of oil. Rub the veal liberally all over with the ground porcini mixture.

**Roast the veal until** it is very tender and nearly falling apart, about 3 hours. Let the meat rest for at least 20 minutes before slicing.

# Ultimate Beef Braciola

It's probably stretching a point to call this a simple supper because it does take a bit of effort to roll and fill the beef. But for a special weekend meal, few things are more delicious, and once you have everything assembled, the cooking is totally hands-off. After the meat is cooked, the savory tomato bath is pureed to make an almost instant sauce.

**Place the panko in** a dry skillet and drizzle with a 1-count of olive oil. Toss over medium heat until golden, 8 to 10 minutes.

**Preheat the oven to 350°F.** Mince the garlic, toasted panko, and parsley and stir to combine.

**Place the flank steak** on a large piece of plastic wrap with the grain running perpendicular to you. Make a long horizontal cut into the edge of the steak almost all the way through and open it up like a book. Lay another piece of plastic wrap on top. Using the smooth side of a mallet or a rolling pin, gently pound the steak until it's about ½ inch thick; take care not to tear the meat. Discard the top sheet of plastic wrap. Rub the top surface of the meat with olive oil and season with salt and black pepper. Spread the bread crumbs evenly over the meat, leaving a 1-inch border all around. Slice the eggs ¼ inch thick and arrange them over the bread crumbs along with the red peppers, anchovies, and mozzarella. Using the plastic to help you lift the edge of the meat, roll the steak against the grain. Tie the roll in 4 or 5 places with kitchen string to help hold the shape and keep the filling from falling out.

**Make the braising liquid:** Place a roasting pan across 2 burners and heat over medium heat. Add a 3-count of olive oil then add the garlic and thyme. Cook for about 1 minute, until fragrant. Carefully add the braciola and sear for about 2 minutes on each side so it is evenly browned all over. Add the sliced onion and bay leaf to the pan, then pour in the beef broth and stir to loosen any browned bits from the

*(continued on page 59)*

## Serves 6 to 8

1½ cups panko bread crumbs

Extra-virgin olive oil

2 garlic cloves

3 tablespoons minced fresh flat-leaf parsley

2 pounds flank steak

Kosher salt and freshly ground black pepper

3 large eggs, hard-boiled and peeled

½ cup chopped jarred roasted red peppers

2 anchovy fillets

1 small ball mozzarella, thinly sliced

## *Braising Liquid*

Extra-virgin olive oil

2 garlic cloves, peeled and gently smashed

6 fresh thyme sprigs

1 small onion, sliced

1 bay leaf

1½ cups low-sodium beef broth

1 (28-ounce) can San Marzano tomatoes, with their juices

8 tomatoes on the vine

Kosher salt and freshly ground black pepper

2 tablespoons good-quality balsamic vinegar

½ bunch fresh flat-leaf parsley, chopped

bottom of the pan. Add the canned tomatoes and their juices, then nestle the fresh tomatoes around the braciola. Bring the liquid to a simmer. Cover the entire pan with foil and place in the oven to braise for 50 to 60 minutes, or until the internal temperature of the beef reads 160ºF on an instant-read thermometer.

**Transfer the braciola** and tomatoes to a platter using a slotted spoon. Discard the thyme stems, tomato stems, and bay leaf, then carefully transfer the contents of the roasting pan to a blender and puree until smooth. Return to the pan and bring to a simmer over medium heat. Season with salt and pepper and add a splash of balsamic vinegar.

**To serve, remove the** kitchen twine from the beef and cut crosswise into 1-inch-thick slices. Serve with some of the sauce ladled on top and sprinkled with parsley.

# Herb-Crusted Crown Roast of Pork

### with APPLE and PECAN STUFFING and CALVADOS GRAVY

When I first tested this recipe for the book, I delivered the final dish to our neighbors, the Buchbinders. They had a house full of family visiting their new son, Rhys, and we conducted an informal tasting. It was a hit, and they served it again as leftovers; they said it was even better the next night. This recipe turned out just the way I envisioned it; the stuffing is perfect for pork.

**Make the stuffing: Set** a large skillet over medium heat and add 3 tablespoons olive oil, the garlic, sage, and thyme. As the oil heats, the herbs will crackle and infuse the oil with flavor. Use tongs to remove the sage branches and set aside on a paper towel to drain; these will be used as a garnish. Add the onions to the pan and cook slowly over medium heat until caramelized, about 15 minutes. Season with salt and pepper and transfer to a bowl. Add the apple slices and pecans to the skillet. Gently sauté over high heat until the pecans are lightly toasted and the apples are slightly cooked, 3 to 5 minutes.

**In a large mixing** bowl, whisk together the eggs, cream, and chicken broth. Add the bread, caramelized onions, apples, pecans, and parsley. Use a wooden spoon to mix the stuffing well. Season with salt and pepper and finish with a drizzle of olive oil.

**Preheat the oven to 375°F** and adjust a rack to the bottom third of the oven. Place a roasting rack inside a large roasting pan.

*(continued on page 62)*

## Serves 12 to 14

### Stuffing

Extra-virgin olive oil

1 garlic clove, peeled and smashed

1 bunch fresh sage

4 fresh thyme sprigs

2 large onions, roughly chopped

Kosher salt and freshly ground black pepper

3 Granny Smith apples, peeled, cored, and thinly sliced

1½ cups chopped pecans

2 large eggs, lightly beaten

¾ cup heavy cream

1½ cups low-sodium chicken broth

5 cups hand-torn sourdough bread pieces, crusts removed

½ cup roughly chopped fresh flat-leaf parsley

### Crown Roast

¼ cup fresh thyme leaves, roughly chopped

¼ cup fresh sage leaves, roughly chopped

5 garlic cloves, minced

Kosher salt and freshly ground black pepper

Extra-virgin olive oil

10-pound pork crown roast (about 12 to 14 ribs), frenched and tied

Calvados Gravy (page 62)

**Prepare the roast:** In a small bowl, combine the thyme, sage, garlic, and salt and pepper to taste. Add enough oil to moisten, and stir to combine. Using a brush, smear the roast all over with the herb paste, covering all surfaces.

**Place the roast on** the rack in the roasting pan, and fill the cavity with the apple-pecan stuffing. Cover the tips of the rib bones with foil, then place the pork in the oven and roast for 2½ hours, or until a meat thermometer inserted near the bone reads 150°F. Check the stuffing after 1½ hours, and cover with foil if it becomes too dark.

**Remove the pan from** the oven and transfer the meat to a cutting board to rest for 30 minutes while you make the Calvados gravy. Cut between the bones to carve the roast into individual chops.

# Calvados Gravy

**Makes 3½ cups**

2 medium carrots, peeled and roughly chopped

1 large onion, roughly chopped

3 celery stalks, roughly chopped

1 turnip, peeled and chopped

1 large Granny Smith apple, peeled, cored, and chopped

1 garlic clove, peeled

Extra-virgin olive oil

2 tablespoons all-purpose flour

1 quart low-sodium chicken broth

Kosher salt and freshly ground black pepper

1 cup Calvados or other apple brandy

4 tablespoons (½ stick) cold unsalted butter, cut into cubes

**Place the carrots, onions,** celery, turnip, apple, and garlic in a food processor and pulse to make a coarse puree.

**Place the roasting pan** with the pork drippings on the stovetop over medium-high heat. Add a 2-count of olive oil and the vegetable puree. Cook gently for 7 to 8 minutes, until most of the moisture has cooked off. Sprinkle the puree with the flour and cook for 2 more minutes, stirring well to incorporate the flour with the fat in the pan.

**Gradually add the chicken** broth, stirring as you go to ensure there are no lumps. Bring to a simmer and season well with salt and pepper. Add the Calvados, and continue to simmer for another 20 minutes.

**Strain the gravy through** a sieve into a saucepan, but don't use a very fine sieve, as allowing some of the pulp to pass through will help to thicken the sauce. Add a few of the cold butter cubes at a time, and swirl to dissolve them, repeating until all the butter has been incorporated and the sauce is thick, velvety, and rich.

# Salads & Sides

# Roasted Kale Chips

I first had kale chips at Blue Hill, Dan Barber's place in New York, and was fascinated by them. I tried frying up my own but I could never seem to replicate them. Then one night, we curled up in front of the fire to watch a movie and Tolan handed me a huge bowl of fresh kale chips. You should have seen the look on my face when she explained the secret was roasting them in the oven. Sometimes she gets fancy and dusts them with a little Parmesan cheese and truffle salt.

**Serves 8 to 10**

3 bunches kale, such as dinosaur kale, curly kale, or a mixture

Extra-virgin olive oil

Sea salt and freshly ground black pepper

**Preheat the oven to 325°F.**
Line a rimmed baking sheet with parchment paper. Wash and dry the kale very well. Cut the kale into chip-size pieces, discarding the thick stems, and arrange on the baking sheet. With a pastry brush, gently paint the top of each kale chip with a little oil, then sprinkle with salt and pepper. Bake until crispy, 30 to 35 minutes.

# Fall Salad

*with* BALSAMIC VINAIGRETTE

Now that we live in California, I can grow more than just a potted tomato plant or two, and I love it. A lot of people just let their garden go once the last basil plant of the summer goes to seed, but I like to plant winter lettuce crops like mustard greens, chicories, tardivo, and kale to supplement fall greens like endive and frisée. The slightly sweet dressing balances out the salad and highlights the "good bitter" flavor of the greens. It's a nice patch of sun in the chilly winter season.

**Make the candied pecans:** Line a baking sheet with wax paper. Combine the butter, brown sugar, and salt in a nonstick skillet over medium heat. When the butter has melted, toss in the pecans and cook, tossing occasionally, for about 3 minutes. Transfer to the baking sheet and use two forks to separate the pecans. Set aside to cool.

**Make the vinaigrette:** In a large mixing bowl, combine the shallot, mustard, and balsamic vinegar. Slowly drizzle in the olive oil, whisking constantly until well combined. Add the honey and Parmesan and season to taste with salt and pepper.

**Add the salad greens** and pear slices to the vinaigrette and toss gently to coat with the dressing. Top with Parmesan shavings and candied pecans and serve.

**Serves 4**

*Candied Pecans*

2 tablespoons unsalted butter

2 tablespoons light brown sugar

Pinch of kosher salt

½ cup pecans

*Balsamic Vinaigrette*

1 small shallot, finely diced

1 teaspoon Dijon mustard

2 teaspoons balsamic vinegar

¼ cup extra-virgin olive oil

2 teaspoons honey

¼ cup shredded Parmesan cheese

Kosher salt and freshly ground black pepper

1 Belgian endive, leaves separated

1 bunch tender purple kale

1 large head radicchio, leaves torn

1 head treviso

1 handful arugula

1 red pear, cored and sliced

¼ cup shaved Parmesan cheese

# Asian Potato Salad

## *with* CUCUMBER, DATES, AND ARUGULA

**Think of this as the perfect side dish to serve with anything you are pulling out the soy sauce for, like teriyaki chicken or sesame ribs. Pick up a packet of wonton strips at your local Chinese restaurant.**

**Place the sweet potatoes** in a saucepan with salted water to cover. Bring to a simmer over medium heat and cook for 15 to 20 minutes until just tender; they should still have a little bite. Drain and cool.

**Make the dressing:** Combine the carrot, ginger, vinegar, mirin, soy sauce, sesame oil, and mayonnaise in a blender and puree until smooth. Transfer the cooled potatoes to a bowl and toss with the dressing.

**Combine the arugula,** cucumbers, dates and cilantro in a large mixing bowl. Add the lemon juice and a little salt and pepper and toss well. Top the dressed potatoes with the arugula salad and garnish with the wonton strips.

### Serves 4 to 6

3 large sweet potatoes, peeled and cut into 1-inch cubes

Kosher salt

### *Carrot-Ginger Dressing*

½ cup grated carrot

2 teaspoons grated peeled fresh ginger

2 tablespoons rice vinegar

2 tablespoons mirin (sweetened rice wine)

1 tablespoon low-sodium soy sauce

1 teaspoon toasted sesame oil

½ cup mayonnaise

4 cups lightly packed arugula

½ hothouse cucumber, finely sliced

1 cup pitted and halved dates

1 cup fresh cilantro leaves

2 cups crispy wonton strips

Juice of 1 lemon

Freshly ground black pepper

# Miso-Glazed Bacon and Asparagus

Nothing with bacon wrapped around it can ever be bad and this is a case in point. The snap of the asparagus paired with the sweet of the miso all combined in a little bacon wrapper and roasted in the oven is simple and delicious.

**Serves 6**

24 asparagus spears, bottom 2 inches trimmed

12 smoked bacon slices, halved crosswise

Bamboo toothpicks, soaked in water

¼ cup shiro miso (white miso paste)

½ cup mirin (sweetened rice wine)

1 tablespoon sugar

1 tablespoon fresh lemon juice

1 tablespoon sesame seeds

**Preheat the oven to 400°F.**

**Peel the asparagus stalks** and halve each spear crosswise. Place an asparagus tip and stalk across each bacon strip, then roll them up and secure with a bamboo toothpick, pushing the toothpick through both pieces of asparagus.

**In a small mixing bowl,** combine the miso, mirin, sugar, and lemon juice and whisk to combine. Arrange the asparagus bundles on a rimmed baking sheet, brush with the miso glaze, and bake until the asparagus is crisp-tender, about 10 minutes. Sprinkle with the sesame seeds and bake until the bacon is cooked and slightly crispy around the edges, about 5 minutes longer.

# On Being a Locavore

When it comes to food, the people of Marin County are pretty darn lucky . . . and we know it. We have the benefit of living in the virtual heart of California's bounty, and to ignore that would be a crime. So the concept of being a "locavore," or one who chooses whenever possible to eat locally grown or locally produced food, is of great importance. Now, I certainly didn't invent this concept, and over the past few years I've entered many discussions with colleagues, friends, and family about what it means and how it can best be applied to cooking. And being a locavore doesn't simply stop at addressing the proximity of your food source. Rather, it encompasses, both directly and indirectly, such concepts as sustainability, organic farming, and being "green," among others. This is all important stuff and as I grow as a chef, a businessman, and a father, the impact of these choices takes on greater and greater significance.

CHEF PARKING ONLY

Coined by a Bay Area chef and author named Jessica Prentice in 2005, the term "locavore" has picked up steam in the last few years, and in fact, was chosen by the *New Oxford American Dictionary* as the 2007 word of the year. This concept has become somewhat political of late as some critics have called the movement to eat local, eat organic, and eat sustainably an elitist and impractical pursuit. Look, I get it. I live in foodie ground zero. The best of the best of anything I could ever want to eat literally comes from just around the corner and, thankfully, I have the means to attain it. But not everyone is so lucky. Organic foods are more expensive . . . they just are. And if you live in the middle of Nebraska, come February, that frozen corn-sicle just isn't going to cut it. So, I understand that this concept can seem a bit out of reach for many people. But, the truth is that as long as we all recognize the concept and factor it into our food choices, we're on the right path.

Let's talk about a few things that make the locavore concept important and worth your time to consider. Locally produced foods, those harvested within a 100-mile radius of one's home, have a lesser impact on the environment because of the decreased need for transportation from source to consumer. Another plus for local foods is that they are generally of superior quality, because they get to the consumer very shortly after harvest. Your apple is what an apple should be, and your chicken really tastes like a chicken . . . not like a chicken-a-zoid that's been pumped full of preservatives to keep it "fresh" as it makes its way across the country. Eating local foods also supports local economies, keeping the money cycling through the community. It's very important that our restaurants not only delight our community's collective palate but nourish and enrich the lives of our neighbors as well.

When people turn to local foods, the benefits are felt up and down the food chain, and even if you don't live in a place where you can take full advantage of the idea, I encourage you to think about ways that you can apply the same principles to your family's dinner table. Despite the controversies—organic vs. local, sustainable vs. cost-effective—the bottom line is that we'd all benefit from a locavore way of life. Even if it isn't completely practical for your household all the time, there are bits and pieces of the concept that you can take away from the philosophy, wherever you live.

# Parmesan-Roasted Green Beans

Roasting green beans gives them depth of flavor and complexity just as it does roasted asparagus. A topping of grated Parmesan creates a crisp, frico-like crust.

**Serves 4**

1¼ pounds thin green beans or haricots verts, trimmed

1 cup grated Parmesan cheese

Kosher salt and freshly ground black pepper

**Preheat the oven to 400°F.** Arrange the beans on a nonstick rimmed baking sheet and sprinkle with the cheese. Roast until the cheese melts and forms a crisp shell over the beans, about 10 minutes. Use a spatula to transfer the beans to a platter and season with a little salt and pepper.

# Buttered Turnip Puree

There is nothing better than classic mashed potatoes but I am always looking for another creamy side dish as an alternative. Pureeing turnips with just the right ingredients makes this humble veg so delicious, I even get my kids to eat them. This dish goes really well with everything from pork to chicken and, in the winter, crispy seared fish.

**Serves 4**

3 large turnips, peeled and cut into uniform chunks

1 quart milk

3 fresh thyme sprigs

1 garlic clove, peeled and gently smashed with the side of a knife

½ cup (1 stick) unsalted butter, cut into small cubes

Kosher salt and freshly ground black pepper

**Combine the turnips,** milk, thyme, and garlic in a medium saucepan. Set over medium heat and partially cover the pan. Bring to a gentle simmer and cook for 20 to 30 minutes, until the turnips are tender; the tip of a paring knife should go through without resistance.

**Drain the turnips,** reserving the cooking liquid, and transfer to a food processor (discard the thyme sprigs). Add about 1 cup of the reserved cooking liquid and the butter, season with plenty of salt and pepper, and puree until smooth. Add more of the liquid if necessary. Serve hot.

# Creamed Spinach

*with* ROASTED CIPOLLINI ONIONS *and* TOASTED BREAD CRUMBS

**This dish was a happy accident. I wanted to serve creamed spinach for our family Christmas dinner but make it a bit more special. Roasted onions and the crunch of bread crumbs really take this old warhorse to the next level. Pair it with a simple grilled steak or beef tenderloin.**

**Serves 4 to 6**

2 pounds cipollini onions

Extra-virgin olive oil

1 cup balsamic vinegar

½ cup honey

1 tablespoon unsalted butter

1 onion, minced

2 garlic cloves, minced

4 (12-ounce) bags fresh spinach, stemmed and washed

2 cups heavy cream

1 teaspoon grated nutmeg

Sea salt and freshly ground black pepper

2 cups panko bread crumbs

**Place the unpeeled onions** in a bowl and cover with very hot water. Set aside for 15 minutes to soften the skins. Drain the onions, then peel and pat dry. Heat a large skillet over high heat and add a 2-count of oil. Add the onions and sauté until they are golden brown all over, about 10 minutes. Add the vinegar and honey, reduce the heat to medium, and cook until the mixture has reduced to a syrup and the onions are soft, about 20 minutes.

**Preheat the oven to 400°F.**

**Heat a large pot** over medium heat. Drizzle with a 2-count of oil, add the butter, and stir it around until it melts. Add the onions and garlic and sauté until soft, about 5 minutes. Add the spinach in batches, pushing it down into the pan with a wooden spoon to help it wilt and adding more spinach as soon as there is room in the pot. Cook the spinach until it is dry, then reduce the heat and add the cream and nutmeg. Stir and cook for 10 minutes. Season with salt and pepper.

**Pour the creamed spinach** into a baking dish and top it with the onions and the panko. Bake until the bread crumbs are golden brown, about 15 minutes. Serve hot.

# Potatoes Savory and Sweet

One Thanksgiving I accidentally used a spoon covered in sweet potato puree to stir the mashed potatoes. I thought that I had made a horrible mistake until I tasted it, and it was so good that I blended both together on the spot. Of course, you could go old-school and serve the purees on their own, either individually or together.

**Preheat the oven to 400°F.**

**Slice off the top** ⅓ of the head of garlic, exposing the cloves. Place the garlic on a square of foil and drizzle with a bit of oil. Fold the foil around the garlic and roast for 30 to 35 minutes until soft. The roasted garlic can be stored in the refrigerator for up to 1 week.

**Place the Yukon Gold** potatoes in a large saucepan with the bay leaf. Add salt, and fill the pan with enough water to cover the potatoes. Place the sweet potatoes in a second saucepan, season with salt, and add water to cover. Bring both pans to a boil over medium heat and cook the potatoes for 20 to 25 minutes, until tender.

**In a microwaveable** measuring cup, combine the cream with the butter and garlic. Heat on high until hot but not boiling. Drain the Yukon Gold potatoes well, and pass through a food mill or ricer. Return the potatoes to the pan and add half of the hot cream mixture. Stir gently to incorporate, then season well with salt and pepper and a drizzle of extra-virgin olive oil. Set aside.

**Drain the sweet potatoes** and place in a food processor along with the bananas, honey, orange zest, cinnamon, and the remaining cream mixture. Process until smooth, working in batches if necessary. Season with salt and pepper.

**To serve, fold the** mashed potatoes and sweet potatoes together gently to combine.

## Serves 4

1 head garlic

Extra-virgin olive oil

3 large Yukon Gold potatoes, peeled and quartered

1 bay leaf

Kosher salt

1 pound sweet potatoes, peeled and cut into large cubes

1½ cups heavy cream

4 tablespoons (½ stick) unsalted butter

Freshly ground black pepper

2 ripe bananas

2 tablespoons honey

1½ teaspoons grated orange zest

1 teaspoon ground cinnamon

# Lemon Smashed Yukon Potatoes

We eat a lot of sole on the West Coast because it is local, fresh, and my wife Tolan's favorite. In my search for the perfect side dish, I tried this one and it stuck. The lemon/Yukon combo goes really well with any kind of mild grilled fish.

**Serves 6 to 8**

8 to 10 medium Yukon Gold potatoes

1 quart heavy cream

1 quart whole milk

Kosher salt and freshly ground black pepper

Grated zest of 2 lemons

¼ cup chopped fresh flat-leaf parsley

**Put the potatoes in** a large saucepan and add the cream and milk. Bring to a boil, then add 1 teaspoon salt, reduce the heat, and simmer for 20 to 25 minutes, until the potatoes are very tender. Drain, reserving the cooking liquid, then return the potatoes to the pan.

**Add the lemon zest,** season with salt and pepper, and use a potato masher to break up the potatoes. Add about 1 cup of the cooking liquid to just moisten the potatoes. Fold in the chopped parsley, season with salt and pepper, and serve immediately.

# Sweet Corn Polenta

## with FENNEL OLIVE SALSA VERDE

Pureed corn kernels makes this polenta especially smooth and creamy. I like to dress it up with a bit of tangy salsa verde, but it's just fine served on its own.

**Serves 4 to 6**

½ cup heavy cream

½ cup milk

Kernels from 2 ears fresh corn (or 1 cup frozen or canned corn kernels)

1½ quarts low-sodium chicken broth

1 teaspoon kosher salt

1½ cups polenta or yellow cornmeal

1½ tablespoons unsalted butter

¼ cup freshly grated Parmesan cheese

1 teaspoon freshly ground black pepper

1 cup Fennel Olive Salsa Verde (below)

**Combine the cream** and milk in a saucepan. Add the corn kernels, bring to a simmer, and cook for 15 minutes. Remove from the heat and let the corn steep in the milk and cream while you make the polenta.

**Bring the chicken broth** to a boil with the salt in a large saucepan. Add the cornmeal gradually in a slow, steady stream, whisking constantly, until thoroughly incorporated. Turn the heat to low and cook for 25 minutes, or until the polenta is smooth and creamy, whisking every 3 to 4 minutes.

**While the polenta** is cooking, drain the corn, reserving the milk-cream mixture. Place the corn kernels in a food processor and puree. After the polenta has cooked for 25 minutes, stir in the milk-cream and the butter and continue to cook, whisking, for another 5 minutes. Stir in enough of the pureed corn to make the polenta super creamy. Stir in the cheese and pepper and serve hot topped with the salsa.

# Fennel Olive Salsa Verde

**Makes about 1 cup**

¼ cup fennel fronds

¼ cup fresh flat-leaf parsley leaves

¼ cup pitted green olives

2 tablespoons capers, drained

4 anchovy fillets

½ cup extra-virgin olive oil

Juice of 1 tangerine

1 tablespoon red wine vinegar

Kosher salt and freshly ground black pepper

**Chop the fennel fronds,** parsley, olives, capers, and anchovies together on a cutting board with a chef's knife until very finely minced. Transfer to a bowl and stir in the olive oil, tangerine juice, and vinegar. Season with salt and pepper.

# Pickled Donut Peaches

## with STAR ANISE, CLOVE, *and* CINNAMON

Peaches take beautifully to pickling and add some brightness to a winter meal of roast pork. Substitute any regular peaches for the donut peaches if you miss them during their brief season.

**Makes 2 pints**

12 to 14 donut peaches

2 large lemons, very thinly sliced and seeds removed

8 cups white vinegar

2 cups sugar

8 whole star anise

10 whole cloves

2 cinnamon sticks

**Bring a large saucepan** of water to a boil over high heat and fill a large bowl with ice water. Blanch the peaches in the boiling water for 15 seconds, then use a slotted spoon to transfer them immediately to the bowl of ice water to stop the cooking process. Once cool, peel the peaches but leave them whole. Divide the peaches and lemon slices between 2 wide-mouth pint canning jars.

**In a small saucepan,** combine the vinegar, sugar, star anise, cloves, and cinnamon sticks and bring just to a boil over medium heat. Stir to dissolve the sugar, then pour the vinegar mixture over the contents of the jars, filling them to within 1 inch of the rim. Divide the whole spices as equally as possible between the jars. Quickly screw the lids securely in place and let cool to room temperature. Once cool, store the pickled peaches in the refrigerator for up to 1 month.

# Pickled Beets and Apples

We love canning in our house. In the summertime the mountain above us is full of wild blackberries, crab apples, and plums, and there are even a few nectarine and peach trees. As soon as the fruit is at its ripest, we reserve a whole day and can it all. At the holidays we pull them out of our storage shed to give as gifts.

**Makes 2 pints**

1½ pounds beets, washed and scrubbed

3 Granny Smith apples

1 medium red onion, peeled and thickly sliced

1 tablespoon whole allspice berries

8 cups white vinegar

1 cup sugar

**Preheat the oven to 375°F.** Wash the beets and wrap individually in foil. Place the beets on a baking sheet and roast for 1 hour and 30 minutes, or until tender when pierced with the tip of a knife (you can poke right through the foil). Let cool.

**When the beets are** cool enough to handle, slip off the skins and slice the beets ½ inch thick. Peel and core the apples and cut them into wedges the same size as the beet slices. Divide the beets, apples, onions, and allspice berries between two wide-mouth pint canning jars.

**Combine the vinegar and** sugar in a saucepan and bring just to a boil over medium-high heat. Stir to dissolve the sugar, then pour the hot vinegar over the contents of the jars, filling them to within 1 inch of the rim. Screw the lids securely in place and let the jars cool to room temperature. Once cooled, store the pickled beets and apples in the refrigerator for up to 1 month.

# Easy Desserts

# Mango Strawberry Sorbet

We love to make homemade desserts for our kids. This is an easy weeknight treat for those nice summer nights when strawberries are at their peak. You can also freeze the berries in the summertime, and use them year-round.

**Combine the mangoes,** strawberries, lime juice, and honey in a food processor and puree until smooth. Add 8 cups crushed ice and process until finely chopped and smooth. Scoop out into serving bowls and serve garnished with mint leaves.

**Serves 4 to 6**

2 mangoes, peeled and chopped

1 pint strawberries, hulled and sliced

Juice of 1 lime, plus wedges for garnish

½ cup good-quality honey

Mint leaves, for garnish

# Chocolate Tart

You only need a small slice of this rich, dense tart to satisfy a hankering for chocolate. Roll the leftover dough into a log and freeze it, then slice it thinly and bake at 325°F for nearly instant home-baked cookies.

**Make the crust:** In a medium saucepan, melt the butter over low heat. Remove from the heat, add both sugars, and stir to combine. Stir in the flour and set aside to cool for 15 minutes (the dough will still be warm).

**Roll out the dough** on a lightly floured surface to a 12-inch circle, about ¼ inch thick. Carefully roll the dough up onto the pin and lay it inside a 9-inch tart pan with a removable bottom. Gently press the dough into the pan; it is important to fit the dough evenly into every nook and cranny of the pan, especially the scalloped edges. Trim off the excess dough with a knife. Chill the tart shell for 20 to 30 minutes.

**Preheat the oven to 350°F.** Put the tart shell on a sturdy baking sheet so it will be easy to move in and out of the oven. Line the shell with aluminum foil and add pie weights or dried beans to keep the sides of the tart from buckling. Bake the tart shell for 30 minutes. Remove from the oven, remove the foil along with the weights, and use a pastry brush to coat the shell lightly all over with a thin layer of egg white. Return to the oven and bake for another 8 minutes, or until the shell is cooked through and a light golden color, but not browned. (The tart will be cooked further with the filling so you don't want it to get too dark.) Set aside to cool while you make the filling. Reduce the oven temperature to 325°F.

**Make the filling:** Combine the heavy cream and milk in a saucepan and heat over medium-low heat until the mixture just simmers slightly around the edges. Take the pan off the heat, add the chopped chocolate, and stir until it's good and smooth. Add the sugar and salt and whisk until well incorporated. Set aside for 5 minutes to cool slightly. Add the eggs and whisk until completely blended. Pour the filling into the cooled tart shell and bake for 15 to 20 minutes, until the filling is set and the surface is glossy. If you see any bubbles or cracks forming on the surface, take the tart out right away—that means it is beginning to overcook. Transfer to a wire rack to cool and serve warm or at room temperature.

## Serves 6 to 8

### Shortbread Crust

¾ cup (1½ sticks) cold unsalted butter

¼ cup granulated sugar

1 tablespoon confectioners' sugar

2 cups all-purpose flour, plus more for rolling

1 egg white, lightly beaten

### Filling

1 cup heavy cream

½ cup whole milk

8 ounces excellent-quality bittersweet chocolate (70% cacao), chopped

¼ cup granulated sugar

¼ teaspoon salt

2 large eggs, at room temperature, beaten

# Warm and Crusty Date Pudding

I tried this recipe a few years ago when I went up against Paula Deen and Cat Cora on *Iron Chef*. They won, but this recipe stuck with me and is one of my family's favorite desserts. Bake it up in one large soufflé dish or in individual ramekins. The egg whites help make the top of the pudding crusty while the center remains warm and soft, like a cake.

**Serves 8**

2 cups pitted dates (6 ounces)

1¼ cups granulated sugar

1 tablespoon pure vanilla extract

¼ cup heavy cream

4 ounces semisweet chocolate, chopped into pieces

½ cup unsweetened cocoa powder

¼ cup all-purpose flour

6 large egg whites

Confectioners' sugar, for garnish

**Preheat the oven to 375°F** and adjust the oven rack to the middle position. Coat a 1½-quart soufflé dish or eight 6-ounce ramekins with nonstick spray.

**Place the dates in** a saucepan and add ¾ cup water. Bring to a simmer and cook over medium-low heat for 10 minutes, or until the dates are very soft and the water is mostly evaporated. Transfer to a food processor and puree until smooth. Add the granulated sugar and vanilla and process until well blended. Scrape into a large mixing bowl.

**Rinse out the saucepan** and add the cream. Bring to a simmer, then remove the pan from the heat, add the chocolate, and stir until melted. Pour the chocolate into the date mixture and stir until smooth. Sift together the cocoa powder and flour. Fold into the chocolate-date mixture with a rubber spatula until well mixed. In a separate bowl, use an electric mixer to beat the egg whites until they form stiff peaks. Gently fold them into the date mixture until just combined.

**Pour the batter into** the prepared dish or ramekins and smooth the top with a spatula. If using ramekins, set them on a rimmed baking sheet. Bake the ramekins for 20 to 25 minutes, the soufflé dish for 25 to 30 minutes, or until the outside of the pudding is set and crusty looking. Cool until the pudding is just warm, and serve with confectioners' sugar sifted on top.

# Meyer Lemon Cupcakes

## *with* LEMON FROSTING

Meyer lemons are a cross between a mandarin orange and a lemon and they have a unique flavor that I just love. They are readily available in California where I live and in some specialty stores, but if you can't find them, just substitute regular lemons. The cream cheese in this recipe makes the cake dense and moist and offsets the acidity of the lemon.

**Make the frosting:** Combine the cream cheese and 1 cup lemon curd in a mixing bowl. Beat with an electric mixer until light and fluffy, 4 to 5 minutes. Chill until ready to frost the cupcakes.

**Preheat the oven to 325°F.** Line a 12-cup muffin tin with paper liners.

**Make the cupcakes:** Whisk together the flour, lemon zest, salt, and baking powder in a mixing bowl. With an electric mixer on medium-high speed, cream the butter and granulated sugar together until light and fluffy. Beat in the cream cheese and reduce the speed to low. Add the eggs, one at a time, beating until each is incorporated and scraping down the sides of the bowl as needed. Beat in the lemon juice and vanilla.

**Add the flour mixture** to the butter and cream cheese mixture in three batches, beating until just combined. Scoop the batter into the prepared muffin tin, filling each three-quarters full. Bake until a cake tester inserted in the center of a cupcake comes out clean, 25 to 30 minutes. Set the tin on a wire rack to cool completely before removing the cupcakes.

**Spoon the 2 cups** lemon curd into a pastry bag fitted with a medium round tip. Dust the cupcakes lightly with confectioners' sugar. Insert the tip of the pastry bag into the top of each cupcake and fill with a bit of lemon curd. Frost the cupcakes and top with a candied lemon wheel.

**Makes 12 cupcakes**

### *Lemon Frosting*

12 ounces cream cheese, at room temperature

1 cup store-bought lemon curd

### *Cupcakes*

1¾ cups all-purpose flour, sifted

1 tablespoon finely grated Meyer lemon zest

½ teaspoon kosher salt

¼ teaspoon baking powder

¾ cup (1½ sticks) unsalted butter, at room temperature

1 cup granulated sugar

3 ounces cream cheese, at room temperature

3 large eggs, at room temperature

2 tablespoons fresh Meyer lemon juice

½ teaspoon pure vanilla extract

2 cups store-bought lemon curd

Confectioners' sugar, for dusting

Candied Meyer Lemon Wheels (page 100)

# Candied Meyer Lemon Wheels

**Makes 24**

2 cups sugar

2 large Meyer lemons, ends trimmed and sliced ⅛ inch thick, seeds removed

**Bring the sugar and** 2 cups water to a boil in a heavy saucepan. When the liquid is clear and bubbling, reduce the heat to low. Add the lemon slices and simmer until the rinds are translucent, 30 to 35 minutes. Transfer the wheels to baking sheets lined with parchment paper, and let cool completely. Extra wheels can be stored in a container with a tight-fitting lid for up to 1 month in the cupboard.

# Apple Brown Betty

### *with* ICE CREAM

A betty is a classic American dessert made up of a baked pudding layered with spiced fruit and sweetened crumbs. I make this dessert with pears when they are in season and in the summer, I add fresh berries. You can also add currants or golden raisins to mix it up.

**Serves 4**

Unsalted butter, for the ramekins

Granulated sugar, for the ramekins

4 Granny Smith apples, peeled, cored, and cut into thin wedges

Juice of 1 lemon

½ cup packed light brown sugar

½ teaspoon ground cinnamon

Pinch of grated nutmeg

2 tablespoons Calvados

4 slices brioche loaf, cut into small cubes

4 tablespoons (½ stick) unsalted butter, melted

1 pint vanilla-bean ice cream

**Preheat the oven to 375°F.** Grease four 6-ounce ramekins with butter and sprinkle with granulated sugar.

**In a large mixing bowl,** combine the apple wedges, lemon juice, brown sugar, cinnamon, nutmeg, and Calvados and toss to combine. Place the bread cubes in a separate mixing bowl and pour the melted butter over them. Toss to coat the bread with the butter. Place some of the bread cubes in the bottom of each ramekin followed by some of the apple mixture. Repeat to make a second layer, pressing down gently on the fillings to compact slightly. Pour any remaining liquid from the apple bowl over the ramekins.

**Arrange the ramekins** on a rimmed baking sheet and bake until golden and crusty, 40 to 45 minutes. Serve warm or at room temperature topped with a scoop of ice cream.

# Vanilla Poached Pears

Poached pears are the perfect, simple dessert on their unembellished own; add some vanilla ice cream and an easy chocolate sauce and they become poire Hélène, a lot more style for just a bit more effort.

**Combine the sugar,** cinnamon stick, and lemon slices with 5 cups water in a large saucepan. Split the vanilla bean lengthwise and scrape the seeds into the pan, then add the pod as well. Bring to a boil and stir occasionally until the sugar is completely dissolved.

**Peel and cut the** pears in half through the stem. Using a melon-baller, scoop out the cores. Add the pears to the poaching liquid and reduce the heat to a simmer. Cook until the pears are just tender (the tip of a paring knife will go through the flesh of a pear with just a little resistance), about 8 minutes. Remove the pan from the heat and cool the pears in the poaching liquid, about 45 minutes.

**Serve the pears as is,** allowing 2 halves per person, or serve each half topped with a scoop of vanilla-bean ice cream, a little pear-poaching syrup, and warm chocolate sauce drizzled over the top.

### Serves 4 to 8

3 cups sugar

1 cinnamon stick

1 lemon, thinly sliced

1 vanilla bean

4 firm pears, such as Bosc or Bartlett

Chocolate sauce (optional; recipe below)

1 quart vanilla-bean ice cream (optional)

# Chocolate Sauce

### Makes 2 cups

12 ounces bittersweet chocolate, coarsely chopped

1½ tablespoons unsalted butter, cut into pieces

1½ cups heavy cream

**Place the chocolate and** butter in a medium, heatproof bowl. Bring the cream to a boil in a small saucepan, then pour over the chocolate and butter. Stir until smooth and glossy.

# Part 2

# Eating Together:
## *My Friends, Neighbors, and Extended Family*

Nzzz one of us can get by without a support system, and never was that more true than in these challenging times. We all work too much and too hard, and have to keep more balls in the air than ever before. And that's where my extended family comes in.

When Tolan and I made the impromptu decision to move to Mill Valley, we jumped on our little cottage in the woods without doing so much as a once-over on the new neighborhood. Of course, we knew what it looked like from the street but we just kind of went with it on the assumption that our new neighbors would all be great and ready to accept us with open arms. When you think about it, living in New York for all of those years, you come to expect a couple of wacky neighbors here and there. A

mob boss upstairs. Twelve club-kids in the studio next door. And the lady with a hundred cats below. But, Mill Valley is different . . . very different. My new neighborhood is a family sanctuary, a place where people lay down their roots and build their lives, and my new neighbors have turned out to be an amazing group of friends—a new family, if you will. We have each other's backs. Our children play together. We laugh together and, of course, we eat together. We have a mutual interest in maintaining the integrity of our collective sanctuary, and when it comes down to making a house a home, the neighborhood factors in more than I ever could have imagined.

Of course I come by this impulse to bring people around the table naturally. There is a tradition

of Southern hospitality in my extended family that I've carried with me wherever I've lived. My grandmother went by the name Florence Mama, and wow, was she a cook. Most of my memories of growing up in South Carolina involve her cooking, or watching her prepare to cook, or listening to her talking about what she was going to cook. Born and raised out in the Georgia countryside, she instilled in my dad and his siblings the meaning of hard work and taught them to grow fruits and vegetables in their yard for their own family meals. All these years later, I taste good old-fashioned Southern food and I think of her.

Now that we have the good fortune to live near such a close-knit group of friends and family, I always offer to cook for special occasions, be it a birthday, holiday, shower— you name it. By far the most requested meals are those that draw on my Southern roots and some of the family recipes I've collected over the years. We've even made a tradition of throwing a New Year's Day Southern feast. I wake up early to start the collards and black-eyed peas and make the biscuit dough, then just keep cooking throughout the day. By early afternoon the chicken is fried, the family shows up, and we're starting the new year with a fabulous meal together.

# A Good Old-Fashioned Potluck

According to the *Oxford English Dictionary,* the term potluck goes back as far as the sixteenth century and refers to the idea of showing up at somebody's home, sometimes even unannounced, and trying one's "luck" with a serving of whatever might be in the host's pot for dinner that night. Over the centuries, the concept has grown to include the "surprise" element of inviting guests to show up with a dish to pass or share, again hitting on the point of trying your luck at mealtime. Out west, the potluck was a popular concept among traveling cowboys, who contributed to the communal pot when visiting a campsite or ranch. Though the potluck ebbs and flows in popularity from decade to decade, it's remained a mainstay of American social life, from family reunions to church events to political gatherings. At my house, it's a neighborhood bonding experience that helps us feel connected and reinforces the strong sense of community that we share here in Mill Valley.

# Haute Dogs

*with* TARRAGON MUSTARD

Who doesn't love a classic pig in a blanket? This is my updated version of a family favorite. Use any kind of sausage—breakfast sausage, chicken-and-apple sausage, whatever you prefer—and combine it with puff pastry, toasted caraway seeds, and a top-quality mustard for the dip. This is a great dish for large or small groups. We serve it at my kitchen shop during cookbook parties and it is always a big hit.

**Serves 6 to 12**

2 frozen puff pastry sheets, thawed

12 precooked gourmet sausages, any flavor

1 egg, lightly beaten

1 tablespoon caraway seeds

1 tablespoon kosher salt

### Tarragon Mustard

1 cup Dijon mustard

½ cup whole-grain mustard

1 tablespoon chopped fresh tarragon

**Preheat the oven to 350°F.** Line a rimmed baking sheet with parchment paper. Cut the puff pastry in half lengthwise and then cut each strip into 3 equal rectangles.

**Roll each sausage** in one of the pastry rectangles and place on the baking sheet, seam side down. Brush each roll with the beaten egg and sprinkle with the caraway seeds and kosher salt. Bake for 25 to 30 minutes, or until the puff pastry is a beautiful golden brown.

**While the rolls bake,** stir together the mustards and the tarragon in a small bowl. Let the rolls cool for a few minutes, then serve hot with the mustard sauce for dipping.

# Saffron Arancini

## (THE BUCHBINDER FAMILY)

Our next-door neighbor, Nina Buchbinder, is one of my wife's closest friends. Her mother, Augusta, comes to visit a few times a year and cooks for days on end, filling the family's freezer. You can stuff them with cheese, meats, or vegetables or just savor them as is. Needless to say, they freeze perfectly.

**Makes about 75 small balls**

6 cups low-sodium chicken broth

½ teaspoon saffron threads

3 ounces Parmesan cheese rinds

4 tablespoons (½ stick) unsalted butter

2 cups Arborio rice

1 cup freshly grated Parmesan cheese

1 large egg yolk

6 cups all-purpose flour, for breading

12 egg whites, slightly beaten, for breading

8 cups bread crumbs, for breading

Vegetable oil, for deep-frying

**In a medium saucepan,** bring the broth to a boil and add the saffron and the cheese rinds. Turn the heat to very low and keep warm while the saffron releases its beautiful flavor.

**Melt 2 tablespoons of** the butter in a large saucepan over high heat. Add the Arborio rice and immediately reduce the heat to medium-high. Cook the rice for a few minutes, or until the grains are becoming translucent. Add the warm broth, 2 ladlefuls at a time, cooking and stirring continuously until all the liquid has been added. Allow each addition of broth to be absorbed almost completely before adding more. This process will take about 20 minutes. Once the rice is just al dente (don't overcook the rice or it will become mushy), turn the heat off and add the remaining 2 tablespoons of the butter, the Parmesan, and egg yolk. Pour the risotto out onto a baking sheet and let cool until you can handle it with your hands. Roll the rice into balls roughly the size of golf balls.

**Set up your breading** station in 3 separate shallow dishes, with the flour in the first dish, the lightly beaten egg whites in the second, and the bread crumbs in the third. Roll the risotto balls in the flour, then the egg, and lastly in the bread crumbs, setting them on a baking sheet as you go. In a deep, heavy pot, heat about 6 inches of vegetable oil to 350°F. For safety reasons, never fill the pot more than halfway with oil. Working in batches, gently lower the balls into the oil and cook until golden brown, 4 to 5 minutes. Don't cook more than 8 or 10 at a time; this ensures that the oil will stay nice and hot. Use a slotted spoon to transfer the fried arancini to paper towels to drain and keep warm while you fry the remaining rice balls. Serve hot.

# Bean Dip

*with* BACON (DINA MONDAVI)

Dina Mondavi is my buddy, and I make my wine with her family. Her bean dip is delicious and very simple, but the addition of the bacon takes it to another level. Of course, everything is better with bacon.

**Serves 10 to 12**

2 (15-ounce) cans black beans, drained and rinsed

3 or 4 bacon slices

½ medium red onion, chopped

1 jalapeño chile (or to taste), seeded and chopped

½ cup chopped fresh cilantro

1 teaspoon ground cumin

Kosher salt

½ cup of your favorite salsa, plus more to taste

Tortilla chips

¼ cup sour cream

Hot sauce

**Place the black beans** in a food processor and puree until smooth. Set aside.

**In a medium skillet,** cook the bacon until crisp, 5 or 6 minutes. Transfer to a paper-towel-lined plate to drain, leaving the fat in the pan. Add the onions and jalapeño, and cook until the onions are translucent, 3 to 4 minutes. Add the cilantro and cumin and cook for 1 or 2 minutes longer. Add the pureed black beans, salt to taste, and salsa, crumble in the cooled bacon, and stir to combine. Serve with tortilla chips, a bowl of sour cream, and hot sauce.

# Nana Clark's Salad

My mother-in-law, Marjorie Clark, first made an appearance in my book *Tyler's Ultimate* with her potato salad recipe. This is her other signature dish, one we enjoy during the summer at our family cookouts.

**Break the cauliflower** and broccoli heads into small florets and slice them into small chunks. Place them in a large bowl and add the scallions, parsley, onions, and radishes.

**In a separate bowl,** stir together the mayonnaise, lemon juice, mustard, and pepper. Pour the dressing over the vegetables and mix well. Cover and refrigerate for 1 hour before serving.

**Serves 10 to 12**

1 head cauliflower

1 head broccoli

1 bunch scallions, cut into ¼-inch slices

2 cups chopped fresh flat-leaf parsley

1 red onion, sliced

1 bunch radishes, trimmed and quartered

2 cups mayonnaise

¼ cup fresh lemon juice

2 tablespoons Dijon mustard

1 teaspoon freshly ground black pepper

# Chicken, Avocado, and Bacon Salad

## (THE COHEN FAMILY)

Janet and Chuck Cohen are godparents to my children and have the best taste and style of anyone I know. They started making a version of this recipe they found in *Gourmet* magazine years back and it has always remained a staple for them. We substituted rotisserie chicken for ease, but you could also poach your own chicken if you'd like.

**Serves 10 to 12**

### Dressing

1 cup low-sodium chicken broth

¾ cup light cream

½ cup cider vinegar

1 large egg, lightly beaten

1 tablespoon sugar

1 tablespoon all-purpose flour

1 teaspoon ground mustard powder

Kosher salt and freshly ground black pepper

---

1 pound lean slab bacon, medium-diced

2 rotisserie chickens

1 cup minced celery

1 cup minced scallions

2 avocados, peeled, pitted, and sliced

3 heads Bibb lettuce, washed and dried

½ cup flat-leaf parsley, chopped

**Make the dressing:** Combine the chicken broth, cream, vinegar, egg, sugar, flour, and mustard powder in a saucepan and whisk to combine. Bring the mixture to a boil over medium heat, then remove from the heat and strain through a fine-mesh sieve. Season with salt and pepper.

**In a medium skillet,** cook the diced bacon until slightly crisp, 6 to 8 minutes. Transfer to paper towels to drain.

**Pull all of the** meat off the chickens, discarding the skin and bones, and cut the meat into bite-size pieces. Place the chicken in a large bowl along with the celery, scallions, bacon, and avocados and toss gently. Add three-quarters of the dressing and toss again, adding the remainder if it seems dry.

**Line a serving platter** with Bibb lettuce leaves and spoon the chicken salad on top. Scatter the parsley over all.

The first time my Mill Valley neighbors and I came together for a potluck, I'll be honest, I didn't know what to expect. I know that I love to cook and I know that my neighbors like to eat well but I had no idea if they'd really make the effort to go above and beyond the ubiquitous sloppy catchall casserole. (Not to date myself, but I kind of remember the seventies and I've seen some pretty shabby potluck spreads.) Wow, did I underestimate my neighbors. If these people eat like this every day at their own homes, I've got some serious competition as the chef on the block. From the Goldmans' rich and hearty cassoulet to the Tokarskis' incredibly smoky lamb, there was no shortage of good food, good fun, and good (pot) luck. All in all, you couldn't go wrong with any of the potluck dishes and we certainly didn't go wrong when we chose Mill Valley, California, as our new neighborhood.

# Carrot Soufflé

(THE TOKARSKI FAMILY)

This is the recipe that started our neighborhood potluck tradition. The Tokarskis brought this over for an Easter get-together, and we talked about it for weeks afterward. It's light and fluffy and can go with almost anything.

**Serves 6 to 8**

½ cup (1 stick) plus 3 tablespoons unsalted butter, at room temperature

2 pound carrots, peeled and cut into 1-inch chunks

4 fresh thyme sprigs

¼ cup packed light brown sugar

¼ cup granulated sugar

3 large eggs, lightly beaten

3 tablespoons all-purpose flour

2 teaspoons baking powder

1 teaspoon salt

¼ teaspoon grated nutmeg

1 tablespoon pure maple syrup

1 vanilla bean, split

**Preheat the oven to 350°F** and adjust a rack to the center position. Grease a 3-quart baking dish.

**Melt the 3 tablespoons** of butter in a large skillet over high heat, cooking until the butter is just starting to brown around the edges. Add the carrots and the thyme sprigs and cook over high heat until the carrots begin to develop a nice golden brown color, about 15 minutes. Slide the skillet into the oven and roast the carrots until they are very soft, about 25 minutes. Transfer to a mixing bowl and discard the thyme sprigs.

**Add the remaining** ½ cup of butter and the sugars to the carrots and use an electric mixer on medium-high speed to beat the mixture until smooth and fluffy, about 2 minutes. Add the eggs, flour, baking powder, salt, nutmeg, and maple syrup, then use the tip of a knife to scrape the seeds from the vanilla bean into the bowl. Beat on medium until well combined.

**Pour the mixture into** the prepared baking dish and bake for 40 to 45 minutes, or until the top is golden brown. Let rest for 20 minutes before serving.

# Chile Relleno Rice

## (CHRISTINA FLACH)

Our neighbor Christina inherited this recipe from her mom. It's not fancy, but trust me, it is really amazing and everyone at the potluck walked out the door asking for this recipe. Try the leftovers for breakfast the next day.

**Serves 6 to 8**

2 cups cooked white rice

2 cups sour cream

1 can condensed cream of chicken soup

2 (7-ounce) cans diced mild green chiles, drained

2½ cups cubed Monterey jack cheese

Kosher salt and freshly ground black pepper

**Preheat the oven to 375°F.** Lightly grease a 9 by 13-inch baking dish.

**In a large mixing bowl,** combine the rice, sour cream, condensed soup, chiles, and cheese. Mix thoroughly and season with salt and pepper.

Spread the rice in the prepared baking dish and bake for 20 to 30 minutes, until lightly browned.

# Cassoulet

## (THE GOLDMAN FAMILY)

We live in a neighborhood of great cooks, but Jonathan Goldman is by far the most ambitious. His cassoulet is a classic take on this great dish, and it's an ideal one-pot supper for family and friends that's also perfectly portable for a potluck.

**2 days ahead:** Place the beans in a soup pot and add water to cover by several inches. Use a pot that's larger than you think you'll need, as the soaked beans will double in size.

**1 day ahead:** Heat a 2-count of oil in a Dutch oven. Add the bacon and cook over medium heat until the bacon fat is rendered. Add the carrots, celery, and onions and cook on high heat for 7 to 10 minutes, until slightly soft. Add the wine and cook for a minute or two, stirring up the browned bits from the bottom of the pan. Drain the beans and add them to the pan along with the broth. Stir in the tomato paste and bring to a boil, then reduce the heat to low, cover the pot, and simmer the cassoulet for 1½ hours. Then add the garlic, herbs, and salt and pepper and simmer for another

30 minutes. Cool the mixture to room temperature, discard the herb stems, and refrigerate, covered, overnight.

**The day of:** Preheat the oven to 350°F. Lift off and discard the hardened fat from the pot of beans and bring to a simmer over medium heat. While the beans rewarm, brown the sausages in a skillet over high heat for 6 to 8 minutes. Cut the sausages into 2-inch pieces and add to the pot along with the duck confit, nestling them down into the beans. Toss the bread crumbs with the butter and salt and pepper to taste and sprinkle over the beans. Top with the chopped parsley. Bake uncovered for 1½ to 2 hours, or until a nice brown crust forms.

**Serves 6 to 10**

1 pound dried flageolet beans

Extra-virgin olive oil

½ pound slab bacon, diced

1 cup diced carrots

3 celery stalks, medium-diced

1 yellow onion, diced

1 cup dry white wine

4 to 5 cups chicken or veal broth

2 tablespoons tomato paste

8 garlic cloves, peeled and smashed with the side of a chef's knife

4 fresh thyme sprigs

4 bay leaves, fresh if possible

2 fresh rosemary sprigs

Kosher salt and freshly ground black pepper

6 to 8 pork sausages

6 confit duck legs

2 cups fresh sourdough bread crumbs

2 tablespoons unsalted butter, melted

2 tablespoons chopped fresh flat-leaf parsley

# Kafta and Garlicky Hummus

## (THE HIGGINS FAMILY)

Bill Higgins is a restaurateur extraordinaire here in the Bay Area (Bix, the Buckeye Roadhouse, Tra Vigne, Fog City Diner) and I consider him both a mentor and a great friend. He and his wife, Vanessa, a culinary-school graduate, are regulars at our family functions and potlucks.

**In a mixing bowl,** combine the bulgur with 2 cups water. Cover and refrigerate for 1 hour. Pour off any water that has not been absorbed, placing your palm on the surface of the soaked bulgur and pressing to squeeze out the moisture. In a food processor, finely chop the onions, bell pepper, and parsley. Transfer the chopped vegetables to a large mixing bowl and add the bulgur, lamb, salt, pepper, and five-spice powder. Use your hands to blend the mixture thoroughly. If the mixture starts to feel warm, add a piece of ice or two to keep it cold.

**Roll the lamb mixture** into small balls and place on a parchment-lined baking sheet. Flatten the balls slightly. Chill in the refrigerator for 30 minutes.

**Heat a few inches** of canola oil in a wok or frying pan to 400ºF. Fry the kafta, a few at a time, for 1 or 2 minutes, until golden brown. Transfer to a paper-towel-lined plate to drain and keep warm while you fry the remaining kafta.

**To make the hummus:** Combine the garbanzos, garlic, tahini, lemon juice, and salt in a food processor and mix until well blended and creamy. With the machine still running, slowly add the boiling water and continue to blend until the hummus is light and fluffy, about another minute.

**Scrape the hummus into** a serving bowl and drizzle with the olive oil. Top with a sprinkle of paprika.

**Makes 45 to 50 meatballs and 4 cups hummus**

### Kafta

½ cup coarse bulgur wheat

1 medium white onion, coarsely chopped

1 medium red bell pepper, coarsely chopped

1 cup fresh flat-leaf parsley leaves

3 pounds ground lamb

1 teaspoon salt

½ teaspoon white pepper

2 teaspoons five-spice powder

Canola oil, for deep-frying

### Garlicky Hummus

1 (15-ounce) can garbanzo beans, drained and rinsed

5 large garlic cloves, peeled

¼ cup tahini

1 tablespoon fresh lemon juice

1 teaspoon salt

2 tablespoons boiling water

2 tablespoons extra-virgin olive oil

Paprika

# Smoked Lamb

## (THE TOKARSKI FAMILY)

We always know when Chris Tokarski is smoking meat at his house because we can see the smoke wafting out of their yard, up into the redwood trees and down toward our house. It's a signal that it's a good time to call over there to see what's cooking. The goal is to cook this lamb low and slow so it can become really tender and absorb the smoky flavor from the wood chips.

**Serves 6 to 8**

1 cup chopped fresh rosemary

6 garlic cloves, minced

½ cup olive oil

½ cup Dijon mustard

2 tablespoons ground mustard powder

2 tablespoons kosher salt

1 tablespoon freshly ground black pepper

1 boneless leg of lamb, 3 to 5 pounds

3 cups soaked wood smoking chips

**In a medium mixing** bowl, combine the rosemary, garlic, olive oil, Dijon mustard, ground mustard, salt, and pepper and whisk to combine. Place the lamb in a shallow baking dish and, using your hands, rub it all over with the marinade. Cover the dish with plastic wrap and refrigerate for least 2 hours, and ideally overnight.

**Heat a gas grill** to medium. Make a flat pouch out of a double thickness of foil that will fit nicely to one side of your grill. Place the soaked chips in the pouch, poke a couple of holes in the top of the pouch, and place the pouch on the grill. Once the wood chips start smoking, turn the grill to low and lay the leg of lamb on the grates. Grill the lamb for 2½ hours, turning every 30 minutes to cook evenly, until the internal temperature reaches 145°F. Add more soaked wood chips as needed.

**Transfer the lamb to** a cutting board to rest for 20 minutes before slicing ⅛ inch thick.

# Kiki's Famous Coconut Cake

I'm the first one to be skeptical about a recipe based on a boxed cake mix, but trust me when I say this is the best coconut cake I have ever tasted. It comes via Candy DeBartolo, aka Kiki, the mother of my wife's oldest and dearest friend, Nikki. If you love coconut cake, give this one a try. I double the frosting recipe because we like a lot of frosting on our cakes.

**Makes one 9-inch cake**

1 package yellow cake mix (one without pudding included)

1 3.4-ounce package instant vanilla pudding

4 large eggs

¼ cup coconut or vegetable oil

2 cups sweetened shredded coconut

## Frosting

2 cups sweetened shredded coconut

2 tablespoons unsalted butter, at room temperature

8 ounces cream cheese, at room temperature

2 teaspoons whole milk

3½ cups confectioners' sugar, sifted

½ teaspoon pure vanilla extract

**Preheat the oven to 350°F.** Grease three 9-inch round cake pans and dust with flour, tapping out the excess.

**In a large bowl,** combine the cake mix, pudding mix, eggs, oil, and 1½ cups water. With an electric mixer, beat on medium speed until well combined. Stir in the coconut.

**Pour the batter into** the prepared cake pans and bake for 30 minutes, or until a toothpick inserted in the center comes out clean.

**Make the frosting:** Spread the coconut on a rimmed baking sheet. Toast in the oven for 10 minutes, or until lightly browned, stirring once or twice to ensure it browns evenly. Let cool. Combine the butter and cream cheese in a mixing bowl.

Use an electric mixer on medium-high speed to beat until fluffy. Add the milk and beat until smooth. Beat in the confectioners' sugar, then beat in the vanilla. Stir in all but ½ cup of the toasted coconut.

**Place one cake layer** on a cake stand and spread with some of the frosting. Add the 2 remaining layers, spreading frosting between the layers. Frost the top of the cake with the remaining frosting and sprinkle with the remaining coconut. Refrigerate until ready to serve.

# Hi-Hi's Chocolate Chip Cookie Sandwiches

## (TIFFANIE DEBARTOLO)

Our friend Tiffanie went on a quest for the most perfect chocolate chip cookie and, luckily for us, we were drafted as taste testers. This recipe does indeed make the perfect chocolate chip cookie, and the frosting in between takes the cake. Our kids always get a batch for their birthdays.

**Make the cookies:** Preheat the oven to 350°F. Line 2 baking sheets with parchment paper.

**In a mixing bowl,** beat the brown sugar and butter together at medium speed until fluffy. Add the eggs and beat until combined. In a bowl, stir together the flour, baking soda, salt, and cinnamon, then add to the butter mixture and combine. Stir in the chips by hand.

**Drop the dough onto** the prepared baking sheets by rounded 2-inch balls, leaving 2 inches between them. Bake for 10 minutes, or until golden brown. Transfer to a wire rack to cool completely.

**Make the filling:** Combine the butter and shortening in a mixing bowl and beat with an electric mixer on low speed until smooth. Gradually add the confectioners' sugar until combined, then beat in the vanilla. Turn the mixer to high and beat until fluffy.

**When the cookies are** completely cool, spread the smooth sides of half the cookies with a heaping dollop of filling. Top each with a second cookie to make a cookie sandwich.

**Makes 1 dozen**

### Cookies

2½ cups packed light brown sugar

1 cup (2 sticks) unsalted butter, at room temperature

2 large eggs

2½ cups all-purpose flour

½ teaspoon baking soda

¼ teaspoon salt

Pinch of ground cinnamon

2 cups chocolate chips

### Filling

½ cup (1 stick) unsalted butter, at room temperature

½ cup vegetable shortening

2 cups confectioners' sugar, sifted

2 teaspoons pure vanilla extract

# Honey's Brownies

## (MARGE *and* LARRY)

This is not your everyday brownie. My mother-in-law, Marge, makes them using her great aunt Honey's family recipe, and they were the brownies of my wife's childhood. This kind of brownie is much more like a cake and not as dense and gooey as a typical brownie; I think the old-school frosting is the best part.

**Preheat the oven to 350°F.** Grease a 9-inch square pan with butter.

**Melt the chocolate in** a glass measuring cup in a microwave on 50% power at 20-second intervals, stirring between each burst. Stop when the chocolate is nearly melted; the residual heat will finish the job. Set aside to cool for 5 minutes.

**In a mixing bowl,** use an electric mixer to beat the butter and granulated sugar together until fluffy. Add the melted chocolate and combine, then beat in the eggs, milk, and vanilla until smooth. Beat in the flour.

**Spread the batter in** the prepared pan and bake for 30 minutes or until a toothpick inserted in the center comes out clean.

**Make the frosting:** In a medium bowl, sift together the confectioners' sugar and cocoa. In a large bowl, cream the butter until smooth, then gradually beat in the sugar mixture alternately with the evaporated milk. Whisk in the vanilla and salt. Beat with an electric mixer on medium-high until light and fluffy, about 5 minutes. If necessary, adjust the consistency with more milk or sugar.

**When the brownies are cool,** apply a liberal coating of the frosting and cut into squares. Sprinkle some or all of the brownies with the choppped nuts if desired.

### Makes 1 dozen

2 (1-ounce) squares semisweet chocolate

½ cup (1 stick) unsalted butter, at room temperature

1 cup granulated sugar

2 eggs, beaten

¼ cup whole milk

1 teaspoon pure vanilla extract

1 cup all-purpose flour

## *Frosting*

2½ cups confectioners' sugar

6 tablespoons unsweetened cocoa powder

6 tablespoons (¾ stick) unsalted butter, at room temperature

5 tablespoons evaporated milk

1 teaspoon pure vanilla extract

1 teaspoon salt

¾ cup chopped walnuts or pecans (optional)

# My Southern Roots

# Old-Fashioned Pimiento Cheese

*with* CRACKERS *and* CRUDITÉS

Until I took my wife home to South Carolina, she had never heard of pimiento cheese. I marched her straight into Magnolia's to meet my friend Chef Donald Barickman and to get an order of pimiento cheese with flatbread. She is now such a loyal devotee of this dish that my dad served grilled pimiento cheese sandwiches at her baby shower.

**Use an electric mixer** to beat the cream cheese in a medium bowl until light and fluffy. Add the cheddar, pimiento, mayonnaise, and lemon juice and season with salt and pepper. Mix on low speed until just combined. Season with cayenne.

**Scrape the pimiento cheese** into a serving bowl and top with the pecans and sprigs of parsley. Place the bowl on a large platter and surround with the crackers, celery, cucumbers, carrots, and radishes.

## Serves 4 to 6

8 ounces cream cheese, at room temperature

2 cups grated cheddar cheese

½ cup diced pimiento

½ cup mayonnaise

Juice of ½ lemon

Kosher salt and freshly ground black pepper

Pinch of cayenne pepper, or to taste

1 cup pecans, crushed

Fresh flat-leaf parsley sprigs, for garnish

Crackers (Ritz are the traditional partner for pimiento cheese)

4 celery stalks, cut into 2-inch sticks

1 hothouse cucumber, cut into 2-inch sticks

3 carrots, peeled and cut into spears

2 cups halved radishes

1 head fennel, sliced

# Chicken and Dumplings

## Finding a dish that pleases a crowd of adults, picky eaters, and toddlers is hard to pull off, but this dish does the trick every time.

**Make the chicken** and stock: Rinse the chicken under cold water and discard the giblets. Place the chicken, bay leaves, garlic, thyme sprigs, a large pinch of salt, and the peppercorns in a large heavy pot and cover with water. Bring to a boil over medium-high heat, then reduce the heat and simmer, uncovered, for 1½ hours, or until the chicken is tender, skimming the surface several times.

**Transfer the chicken to** a platter to cool a bit and strain the stock through a fine-mesh sieve, discarding any solids. Pull the chicken into big pieces and discard the skin and bones. Cover and set aside. Measure out 6 cups of the chicken stock, reserving any additional stock for another use.

**In a Dutch oven, heat** the butter and oil together over medium heat until the butter melts. Add the carrot, celery, garlic, and bay leaves and cook, stirring, until the vegetables are soft, about 5 minutes. Add the flour and whisk until combined, then continue to stir and cook for 2 minutes. Slowly pour in the 6 cups of chicken stock, 1 cup at a time, stirring

well after each addition. Add the peas and pearl onions. Simmer the sauce until it is thick enough to coat the back of a spoon, about 15 minutes. Stir the heavy cream and reserved shredded chicken into the sauce and bring to a simmer.

**Make the dumplings:** Sift the flour, baking powder, and salt together into a large bowl. In a small bowl, lightly beat the eggs, buttermilk, and chives together; pour the egg mixture into the bowl with the flour and fold together gently, mixing just until the dough comes together. The dough will be very soft.

**Using 2 spoons,** carefully drop heaping tablespoonfuls of the buttermilk-chive dumpling batter onto the hot chicken mixture. The dumplings should not be touching or crowded. Cover the pot and cook the dumplings for 10 to 15 minutes, until they are firm, puffy, and cooked through. Season with freshly ground black pepper and garnish with chopped parsley before spooning the chicken, dumplings, and sauce into shallow soup bowls.

**Serves 4 to 6**

*Chicken and Stock*

1 whole chicken, 4 to 5 pounds

2 bay leaves

1 head garlic, halved horizontally

6 fresh thyme sprigs

Kosher salt

4 to 5 black peppercorns

2 tablespoons unsalted butter

1 tablespoon extra-virgin olive oil

½ cup diced carrot

½ cup diced celery

3 garlic cloves, minced

2 bay leaves

5 tablespoons all-purpose flour

1 cup frozen peas

1 cup frozen pearl onions

¼ cup heavy cream

Freshly ground black pepper

*Dumplings*

2 cups all-purpose flour

1 tablespoon baking powder

1 teaspoon salt

2 large eggs

¾ to 1 cup buttermilk

¼ cup chopped fresh chives

Chopped fresh flat-leaf parsley

# Chicken-Fried Steak

*with* SOUTHERN MILK GRAVY

**This recipe comes from my grandmother, Florence Mama, and it's one of the dishes I crave the most whenever I head back home to South Carolina.**

**Serves 4 to 6**

2 pounds boneless rib-eye steaks, cut ½ inch thick

2 tablespoons table salt, for brine

Vegetable or peanut oil, for frying

4 cups self-rising flour, such as White Lily (see Note)

1 teaspoon paprika

1 teaspoon garlic powder

1 teaspoon onion powder

1 tablespoon kosher salt

1 teaspoon freshly ground black pepper

1 scallion, green part only, chopped

**Using the smooth side** of a meat mallet, gently pound the steaks; this will tenderize the meat and also will create a thinner, faster-frying steak. Place the steaks in a shallow baking dish. Cover with cold water and add the table salt; this is called a brining solution. Cover the dish and refrigerate for at least 2 hours and up to 8 hours. This brining process will give the steaks a wonderful seasoning to them, as well as making them extra juicy.

**In a deep skillet** or heavy, wide pot, heat 4 inches of oil over medium-high heat to 350°F. If you don't have a thermometer, another way to test the oil is to drop in a 1-inch cube of white bread. After 60 seconds of frying it should be golden brown. If the bread burns after 30 seconds, the oil is too hot; if the bread does not brown, the oil is not hot enough.

**In a shallow bowl,** stir together the flour, paprika, garlic powder, onion powder, salt, and pepper until combined. One by one, lift the steaks out of the brining solution, shaking off the excess, and drop them into the seasoned flour. Pat the flour on well, then shake off the excess. Repeat the entire process again, dipping the coated steak back into the brining solution and then back into the flour. (Double-dipping the steaks ensures a nice, thick, delicious crust.)

**Shake off the flour** one last time and gently slip the steaks into the hot oil. Do not fry more than 2 pieces of steaks at a time, as this will lower the temperature of the oil too much, making the crust soggy. Fry the steaks for 10 to 12 minutes on each side. Remove from the oil and let the steaks rest for 10 minutes before cutting. If you like your steak well done, place the fried steaks on a baking sheet and bake in a 400°F oven for 10 to 15 minutes.

*Note:*
If you can't find self-rising flour, replace 3 tablespoons of the flour with 2 tablespoons baking powder and 2 teaspoons salt.

# Milk Gravy

**Makes 3 cups**

¼ cup all-purpose flour

3 cups whole milk

1 teaspoon black pepper

½ teaspoon salt

**To make the gravy:** Pour out all but 2 tablespoons of the oil from the skillet. Add the flour and cook over medium heat, whisking constantly, for about 1 minute. Whisk in the milk and continue to cook, whisking often to prevent lumps, until smooth and thick, about 10 minutes. Season with salt and pepper.

# Buttermilk Biscuits

Another recipe from Florence Mama.
I substitute lard for butter just to make the
biscuits a little over-the-top; the pork fat has
the consistency of clarified butter, and it
makes them much lighter and fluffier.

**Makes 24 biscuits**

4 cups self-rising flour, such as White
Lily, plus more for rolling the dough
(see Note, page 148)

1 cup pork lard, medium-diced and
very cold

4 cups buttermilk

4 tablespoons (½ stsick) unsalted
butter, melted

**Preheat the oven to 375°F.**
Line 2 baking sheets with
parchment paper.

**Place the flour in** a big mixing
bowl. Add the diced cold lard and,
working with your fingers, mix the
lard into the flour until it resembles
small, flour-coated crumbs. Work
quickly; you don't want the lard to
become warm and creamy or your
biscuits won't be flaky. When the
bits of lard are about the size of
small peas, add the buttermilk.
Stir gently with a wooden spoon just
until the dough comes together,
again being careful not to overmix.

Turn the dough onto a floured
surface and knead just until it
comes together. Roll the dough into
a round about 1½ inches thick. Use
a 2-inch biscuit cutter to cut out
24 rounds, and arrange them on
the prepared baking sheets, leaving
2 inches between the biscuits. Brush
the tops with the melted butter and
bake for 10 to 15 minutes, or until
the tops are golden brown.

# Fish Fry-Up

*with* FENNEL SAUSAGE HUSH PUPPIES *and*
BIG PAPA'S TARTAR SAUCE

My dad and I bought an outdoor turkey frying kit and decided to use it to fry up a bunch of fish and hush puppies. It worked just fine and better still, it kept the kitchen from getting splattered with hot cooking oil and hush puppy batter. We threw some newspaper on platters and served everything family style with a couple bowls of tartar sauce. It was a great meal for a big group, and an afternoon of frying over a couple of beers with my dad was the best part.

## Serves 6 to 8

1 pound petrale sole fillets, or other firm white fish

1 pound jumbo shrimp, peeled and deveined

2 pints shucked medium oysters

1½ quarts buttermilk

6 tablespoons Tabasco sauce

8 cups cornmeal

Kosher salt and freshly ground black pepper

Vegetable oil, for deep-frying

Lemon wedges

Big Papa's Tartar Sauce (page 156)

Fennel Sausage Hush Puppies (page 156)

**Place the fish, shrimp,** and oysters in 3 separate shallow bowls. Add enough buttermilk to each bowl to just cover the contents. Add 2 tablespoons of the Tabasco to each of the dishes and combine. Let the seafood marinate in the buttermilk for 30 minutes at room temperature or refrigerate for up to 2 hours.

**Place the cornmeal in** a separate bowl and season it liberally with salt and pepper. Taste the cornmeal to make sure it is well seasoned. Heat several inches of oil to 365°F in a large, heavy pot over high heat; don't fill the pot more than halfway with oil. Remove the fish fillets from the buttermilk marinade, allowing the excess to drip back into the bowl, and dredge each piece in the cornmeal mixture, coating on all sides and shaking off any excess. Carefully place the fish fillets in the hot oil and fry until golden brown, about 8 minutes. Transfer to a paper-towel-lined baking sheet and immediately season with salt and pepper. Keep warm as you bread and fry the shrimp, and then the oysters, cooking the shrimp for 4 minutes and the oysters for about 2 minutes. (Frying one type of seafood at a time ensures that everything cooks evenly.) Don't overcrowd the oil, as that brings down the temperature of the oil, resulting in a soggy fry; and be sure to allow the oil to return to 365°F between each batch. Serve hot with lemon slices and tartar sauce, and with the hush puppies on the side.

# Big Papa's Tartar Sauce

**Makes 4 cups**

2 cups sour cream

2 cups mayonnaise

2 tablespoons dill pickles, finely diced

1 tablespoon drained capers, minced

1 shallot, minced

1 teaspoon chopped fresh tarragon

2 teaspoons Dijon mustard

1 teaspoon Worcestershire sauce

Grated zest and juice of 1 lemon

Kosher salt and freshly ground black pepper

**Combine the sour cream,** mayonnaise, pickles, capers, shallots, tarragon, Dijon mustard, Worcestershire sauce, lemon zest and juice, and salt and pepper to taste in a medium-sized mixing bowl. Stir the ingredients until well combined. Chill until ready to serve.

# Fennel Sausage Hush Puppies

**Makes about 2 dozen**

Extra-virgin olive oil

2 links Italian sausage with fennel seeds

4 cups cornmeal

6 tablespoons self-rising flour, such as White Lily

2 teaspoons kosher salt

¼ cup finely chopped scallions

2 cups buttermilk

2 large eggs, beaten

Vegetable or peanut oil, for deep-frying

**Place a skillet over** high heat. Add a 2-count of olive oil, remove the sausages from their casings and crumble the sausage into the skillet. Brown the sausage for a minute or two to develop flavor, then reduce the heat to medium and stir until the sausage is thoroughly cooked, about 10 minutes. Set aside to cool.

**In a mixing bowl,** combine the cornmeal, flour, salt, and scallions. Add the buttermilk, eggs, and sautéed sausage, and combine thoroughly. Let the batter rest for 10 minutes.

**In a deep fryer** or deep, heavy skillet, heat 4 to 5 inches of peanut oil to 375°F. Gently drop the batter by tablespoonfuls into the hot oil, 6 at a time. Keep an eye on the temperature of the oil; the temperature will drop after you add the batter. If it drops more than 5 degrees, raise the heat a bit until it returns to 375°F. Fry until golden brown, turning several times. Drain on paper towels. Serve hot.

# The Kitchen Shop

Like a driver without a car or a painter without a canvas, I'd be lost without a kitchen. And when I look back at my moves back and forth across the country over the years, I think of many past abodes in terms of how I set up the kitchens. From piecing together a set of utensils at my mom's place as a teenager to using my New York City apartment as the set for the original *Tyler's Ultimate*, every kitchen represents a distinct stage in my progression as a chef.

When we got to California, Tolan and I went about setting up the kitchen in our new cottage in the redwoods like a couple of kids playing house. We had tons of ideas on how it should look, feel, and smell. And I'd like to tell you that it is completely finished but truth be told, I'll be working on this kitchen for as long as I live here! But what became abundantly clear to Tolan and me through the process of building our first kitchen together was how passionate we both were about what a kitchen should mean to a home—and how much we felt we could help others create their own kitchens. We're pretty lucky to be able to travel the world and visit kitchens of all shapes and sizes, from the ultramodern to the most rustic and historic, and we've found inspiration in them all. When we learned that Mill Valley's only kitchen shop had recently shut down, we jumped on the opportunity to put that knowledge to work. So Tolan and I set out to open our very own mom-and-pop shop—and our first brick-and-mortar business—Tyler Florence West Coast Kitchen Essentials, aka the Tyler Florence Shop. (I know, I know, I really went deep to find that one.)

TYLER FLORENCE · MILL VALLEY

When we went looking for the perfect spot for our little shop, we really only had one address on our radar: 59 Throckmorton in Mill Valley was home to the original Banana Republic, the Ziegler family's very first storefront. Eventually the chain, which was sold to Gap, Inc., changed concept and moved on; eager to capture the good juju that comes with a location like that, I jumped at the chance to take it over. Within four months, all the kitchen wisdom accumulated from my years of traveling, cooking, thriving, and surviving in kitchens of all descriptions found an outlet in one glorious shop. Not surprisingly, this too has become a family affair: Marge and Janet (Tolan's mother, Marge, and godmother, Janet,) relentlessly and meticulously

tending the ever-evolving cookbook library; and Larry and Chuck (their less great-looking halves) diligently supervising the wine fridge. Jim creates masterful seasonal window displays and Daniel gives crunching numbers a reality check. JJ, Tamara, Charlie, and Kathy hold down the sales floor each and every day, and Antonia makes sure it looks beautiful every morning when we walk in.

Every few weeks, the shop family throws a party for our favorite customers and local friends to show our appreciation for their support. An evening at the shop can be anything from a book signing with my friend Ina Garten, the Barefoot Contessa, to a burger cook-off with San

Francisco's own chef Hubert Keller. Whatever the event, we have a lot of fun; we share fantastic food and work together to make sure everybody has a great time. It takes all hands on deck and I like to think that a few laughs and a few delicious bites make it as rewarding for the shop family as it is for Tolan and me.

The Mill Valley shop has been such a hit that we are already busting out of our mom-and-pop mold, with an outpost of the shop at San Francisco Airport and another on the way in downtown Napa's new Riverfront development. The shop is going to be gorgeous and will be adjacent to my first fast-casual restaurant, Tyler Florence Rotis-serie and Wine Bar. I'm really excited about this combo in Napa, as you'll be able to check out the shop and then pop next door to grab a glass of TF Pinot and some delicious rotisserie chicken, lamb, or porchetta, among other market-fresh offerings. And who knows where that kitchen experience will take me next?

# Black-Eyed Peas

*with* STEWED TOMATOES

Every New Year's Day we do a big Southern Fried Chicken Feast at our house. I wake up early to put the black-eyed peas on the stove and let them stew all day. By the time the kids wake up, I'm ready for them to help me cut the biscuits. It's become a family tradition that I look forward to every year.

**Serves 4 to 6**

2 pounds dried black-eyed peas

1 large smoked ham hock, about 1 pound

1 quart low-sodium chicken or vegetable broth

½ cup (1 stick) unsalted butter

2 (15-ounce) cans whole San Marzano tomatoes, with their juices

1 white onion, coarsely grated

3 garlic cloves, finely chopped

¼ cup sugar

Leaves from 2 fresh oregano sprigs, finely chopped

1 cup chopped fresh flat-leaf parsley

Kosher salt and freshly ground black pepper

**Place the peas in** a bowl with water to cover by at least 3 inches. Soak the beans at room temperature for at least 4 hours and preferably overnight.

**Preheat the oven to 350°F.** Place the ham hock in a baking dish and roast for 30 to 40 minutes, until browned all over.

**Drain the soaked peas** and place in a large heavy pot. Add the chicken or vegetable broth and nestle the roasted ham hock in the center of the pot. Bring to a boil, then reduce the heat and simmer over low heat, uncovered, until the peas are tender, about 1 hour.

**While the peas cook,** melt the butter in a large, heavy saucepan. Add the tomatoes, onion, garlic, and sugar. Cook over medium heat, stirring often, until thick and reduced, about 30 minutes.

**Just before serving, stir** the oregano and parsley into the tomato sauce and season with salt and pepper. If desired, shred the meat from the ham hock and stir into the peas. Add the tomato sauce to the peas, stir to combine, and serve. Serving the peas from the pot they were cooked in is always a nice touch.

# My Bread-and-Butter Pickles

The longer these sit the better, but if you slice the cukes really thin on a mandolin, they will be pretty delicious in just a few hours.

**Slice the unpeeled** cucumbers ¼ inch thick. Combine the sliced cucumbers, onions, and salt in a large bowl. Cover with about 2 inches of ice cubes and refrigerate for 3 to 4 hours, adding more ice as it melts. Drain the vegetables in a colander and rinse under cold water.

**In a large pot,** combine the sugar, vinegar, and spices. Bring to a gentle simmer over medium heat but do not boil. Simmer for 10 minutes, then add the cucumbers and onions. Heat until the mixture returns to a gentle simmer, then immediately remove from the heat. Cool, then transfer to covered containers and store in the refrigerator for up to 1 week.

**Makes 2 quarts**

2 pounds Kirby cucumbers

2 medium white onions, sliced

¼ cup kosher salt

1 cup sugar

1 cup white vinegar

4 whole cloves

1 tablespoon mustard seeds

½ tablespoon celery seed

¼ teaspoon ground turmeric

# Big Papa's Banana Pudding

As kids, my brothers and I used to fight over the last of this addictive pudding, and my kids love it now as much as I did then. The brûléed meringue on the top makes for an impressive presentation. My dad, "Big Papa," serves this dessert weekly when he cooks for his church congregation.

**Serves 6 to 8**

2 cups half-and-half

¾ cup granulated sugar

½ cup all-purpose flour

½ teaspoon salt

3 egg yolks

2 tablespoons unsalted butter, at room temperature

2 tablespoons pure vanilla extract

2 egg whites

¼ teaspoon cream of tartar

½ teaspoon pure vanilla extract

¼ cup confectioners' sugar

1 (12-ounce) box vanilla wafer cookies

3 ripe bananas, sliced ¼ inch thick

**Make the pudding:** Combine the half-and-half and granulated sugar in a stainless-steel bowl or the top of a double boiler set over simmering water. Whisk in the flour and salt until they combined, about 2 minutes, then remove from the heat. Place the egg yolks in a separate bowl and gradually add half of the hot cream mixture while stirring constantly to temper the eggs. Whisk the egg mixture into the remaining hot cream and place back over the simmering water. Cook, whisking constantly, until the mixture has thickened to the consistency of a thin pudding, about 10 minutes. Remove from the heat and stir in the butter and vanilla. Set aside to cool for 20 minutes; it will continue to thicken as it cools.

**Make the meringue:** Beat the egg whites in a bowl with an electric mixer for 1 minute. Add the cream of tartar, vanilla, and confectioners' sugar, and beat on medium-high speed until the whites form stiff peaks. Preheat the broiler.

**To assemble the pudding,** cover the bottom of a 2-quart glass baking dish with vanilla wafers. Top with half the banana slices and half the cooled pudding. Make a second layer, ending with the pudding. With a spatula, spread the meringue over the entire banana pudding, forming attractive peaks. Slide the dish under the broiler until the meringue is golden brown on top, 2 to 3 minutes.

# Part 3

# Eating Out:
## *My Restaurant Families*

**M**ill Valley, in Marin County, is a remarkable community and I love being a part of it. But, that said, I don't know that I would feel the same about my adoptive hometown without the great city of San Francisco just fifteen minutes to the south. San Francisco holds a very special place in the hearts of many and has a rich culinary history to rival that of any world capital. No wonder it's home to some of the most spectacular restaurants in the country.

So it seemed like a natural evolution in my career to realize my dream of opening my own restaurant once I'd made the Bay Area my home—so much so, in fact, that I launched not one but three different restaurant concepts this year: Wayfare Tavern, a elegant space in the financial district that pays tribute to the golden era of San Francisco fine dining; El Paseo, a neighborhood gathering spot featuring local produce and products; and Tyler Florence Rotisserie and Wine in Napa, a storefront operation that is all about making great meals available at a great price. It's been exciting (and a little humbling) to join the rank of chefs like Michael Mina, Hubert Keller, Judy Rodgers, Traci Des Jardins, Gary Danko, and so many other culinary heavyweights who preside over restaurant kitchens here in the Bay Area and to meld my kind of updated comfort food with the amazing ingredients and artisanal sensibility that are so prevalent here.

The culinary traditions of San Francisco started more than a century and a half ago, during the days of the Gold Rush when the cry of "Gold"

rang around the world and wanderers, thrill-seekers and treasure hunters from all corners of the earth sailed into San Francisco Bay in pursuit of the mother lode. Many of their sailing vessels, left abandoned in the bay, were converted into the city's earliest restaurants. And the ships' cooks commandeered their own piece of the pie by feeding the gold hunters who congregated for food, drink, and good times. These wayfarers had new money to spend and were looking for a party; those early chefs from Italy, France, Spain, Mexico, China, and Japan set out to provide just that, inspiring the great bohemian spirit of San Francisco that lives on today.

The Barbary Coast, as the downtown area became known, definitely had its share of debauchery, but a sophisticated international dining scene was developing in its midst, with spots like Marchand, the

Delmonico, Perini's, the legendary Palace Hotel, and the beachside Cliff House. Each restaurant had its own character and spoke to the origins of its owners and of the various locals who frequented it. One of the more unique spots of the era was the funky Cobweb Palace at Meigg's Wharf. It was a ramshackle building filled with curios from around the world including taxidermied bears, monkeys, parrots, cats, and dogs piled indiscriminately on boxes and barrels and covered in dust and cobwebs. Abe Warner, the eccentric proprietor, served up beautiful local crabs and clams in a variety of preparations. And in the back room, he prohibited the sale of such mainstream liquors as whiskey in favor of more sophisticated imported fare like French brandy, Spanish wines, and English ales. What I wouldn't give to grab a drink and some steamed Dungeness crab at that joint!

It was a vibrant period of growth and creativity in San Francisco that was briefly interrupted by the Great Quake of 1906, which reduced it all to rubble and burned dreams. But the early San Franciscans were resilient; within days these hardy folks began the earliest form of what in current culinary argot are called "pop-up" restaurants, as they threw together small shacks to continue the great culinary traditions of the city. Restaurants rebuilt, great chefs continued to come from all over the world, and it just got better and better. Today, a century and half after it all began in the hulls of some abandoned ships, San Francisco lives on as one of the greatest culinary cities in the world, and I am proud to be part of its future. The menus at my three restaurants—Wayfare Tavern in San Francisco; El Paseo in Mill Valley, and the Rotisserie and Wine

Bar in Napa—all have their own unique character yet each in its own way expresses the spirit of the region in all its colorful variety.

The recipes in this section are representative of what you'll find on those menus, from contemporary reinterpretations of amazing classic dishes at Wayfare to market-inspired meals at El Paseo. They may be a little more involved than the meals I make at home or may feature an extra component (most of which can be made ahead of time) but at heart they are really not that different; they are my way of making everyone who passes through my doors feel like family.

# Soups & Starters

# Warm Olives and Cipollini Onions
## *with* HONEY GASTRIQUE

I love olives, and this amazing mixture of flavors "rolls" across your palate, hitting spicy, sour, salty, and sweet notes all at once. Opening up the taste receptors with a smart bite before a meal is like stretching your hamstrings before a 10-K run. You can halve or even quarter this recipe.

**Place the unpeeled onions** in a large bowl. Pour a few cups of extremely hot tap water over the onions and set aside for 15 minutes to loosen the skins. Drain the onions and peel; pat dry.

**Place a very large** skillet over high heat and add a 2-count of olive oil. Add the peeled onions and the salt and sear until the outsides are nice and golden brown, 5 to 7 minutes. While the onions brown, combine the vinegar, honey, and 2 tablespoons of olive oil in another skillet and bring nearly to a simmer over low heat. Add the bay leaves, rosemary, zests, garlic, and olives. Once the onions are nice and golden brown, carefully pour in the olive mixture. Simmer over low heat, uncovered, for 30 to 35 minutes, or until the onions are cooked through and the liquid has reduced slightly and has a syrupy consistency. Serve warm.

### Makes about 2 quarts

½ pound small cipollini onions, halved

2 teaspoons kosher salt

Extra-virgin olive oil

3 cups sherry vinegar

2 cups good-quality honey

2 fresh bay leaves

1 large fresh rosemary sprig

Grated zest of 1 orange

Grated zest of 1 lemon

5 garlic cloves, peeled and smashed with the side of a chef's knife

1 pound unpitted mixed olives

# Deviled Eggs

## with ANCHOVIES, CAPERS, *and* PIMENTÓN

Deviled eggs are one of my favorite appetizers and with the right garnish they take on a very polished look and taste. The neutral richness of the yolk absorbs flavors very well.

**Makes 2 dozen**

2 bacon slices

12 eggs

¼ cup mayonnaise

4 tablespoons drained capers

2 tablespoons Dijon mustard

3 anchovy fillets, minced

2 teaspoons smoked paprika (pimentón), plus more for dusting

1 teaspoon kosher salt

1 cup vegetable oil, for frying

Celery leaves, for garnish

**Cook the bacon in** a small skillet until crisp, 4 to 5 minutes. Drain on paper towels and, when cool, crumble coarsely.

**To make perfect** hard-boiled eggs, place them in a saucepan of cold water and bring the water to a boil over high heat. Once the water boils, immediately shut off the heat and let the eggs sit in the water for exactly 14 minutes. Transfer to a bowl of cold water and peel the eggs.

**Halve the eggs lengthwise** and gently scoop the yolks into a food processor. Add the mayonnaise, 2 tablespoons of the capers, the mustard, anchovies, pimentón, and salt. Pulse until smooth. Transfer the filling to a pastry bag fitted with a ¼-inch plain round tip or to a resealable plastic bag with a small bit of the corner snipped off. Neatly pipe the yolk mixture into the egg whites.

**Heat the vegetable oil to 375°F** in a small skillet. Drop in the remaining 2 tablespoons of capers and fry until crispy, about 4 minutes. Use a slotted spoon to transfer to a paper-towel-lined plate to drain. Garnish the eggs with the crispy capers, bacon, celery leaves, and a bit of smoked paprika.

# Grilled Artichokes

*with* SAUCE GRIBICHE

California's artichokes are as good as any
I've had in Italy, France, or Spain—and maybe
even better. Grilling is my new favorite way to
cook artichokes; the smoky, slightly charred,
crunchy artichoke houses a soft, tender heart
that gets a lift from a creamy, rich sauce made
from hard-boiled eggs, chopped herbs, and
lots of salty bits.

**Make a medium fire** in your
charcoal grill or preheat a gas grill to
low. Rub the artichoke halves with
2 tablespoons of the olive oil and
season with salt and pepper. Grill cut
side down over low heat or slightly
away from the coals if using a
charcoal grill, until the artichokes
are soft, about 20 minutes. Turn the
flame to medium-high or move the
artichokes over the hottest part of
the coals for 5 minutes to give them
some color, then transfer to a platter.

**Preheat the oven to 375°F.**

**While the artichokes** are grilling,
spread the bread crumbs on a
rimmed baking sheet and drizzle
with the remaining tablespoon of oil.
Toss to combine, then spread them
evenly on the sheet. Toast for 12 to
15 minutes, stirring once or twice,
until golden.

**Make the sauce gribiche:**
Combine the mayonnaise, yogurt,
pickles, parsley, capers, shallots,
thyme, eggs, lemon juice, and salt
and pepper to taste in a mixing
bowl. Stir until thoroughly incorporated. Drizzle some of the sauce into
the cavity of each artichoke and top
with the bread crumbs.

**Serves 4 to 6**

3 large globe artichokes, cut in half
lengthwise

3 tablespoons extra-virgin olive oil

Kosher salt and freshly ground
black pepper

1 cup panko bread crumbs

## *Sauce Gribiche*

1 cup mayonnaise

1 cup plain yogurt

3 tablespoons finely chopped
dill pickle

2 tablespoons minced fresh flat-leaf
parsley leaves

2 tablespoons chopped drained
capers

1 tablespoon minced shallot

1 teaspoon finely chopped fresh
thyme leaves

2 hard-boiled eggs, peeled and finely
chopped

Juice of 1 lemon

Kosher salt and freshly ground
black pepper

# Grilled Calamari

### *with* SMOKED OLIVE OIL *and* LEMON CONFIT

Calamari, or fresh squid, is so neutral in taste that it's the perfect vehicle for a flavor road trip. This trip we're headed to California with Meyer lemon confit and one of my favorite new ingredients, smoked olive oil. Made from olives that are cold-smoked before they are crushed, it's one of the sexiest flavors I've come across in years. Genius. You can pick some up at thesmokedolive.com.

**Serves 10 to 15**

1 pound cleaned calamari

1 cup smoked olive oil, or best-quality extra-virgin olive oil

Sea salt and freshly ground black pepper

2 cups panko bread crumbs

1 tablespoon extra-virgin olive oil

¼ cup Meyer Lemon Confit (opposite page)

12 fresh fennel fronds or chervil sprigs, for garnish

**Rinse and dry the** calamari very well and place in a resealable plastic bag. Add the smoked olive oil, turn to coat, and marinate in the refrigerator for 2 hours, or up to overnight.

**Make a very hot** charcoal fire or preheat your gas grill to high. Drain the calamari, discarding the marinade, and pat dry with paper towels. Season with sea salt and pepper. Fold a double thickness of paper towels in quarters and use them to wipe the grill grates with oil; this will prevent the food from sticking. Place the calamari on the grill and cook for just 1½ minutes per side or until it has a bit of char; don't overcook or the calamari will become rubbery. Let rest for 1 minute, then separate the tubes and tentacles, slicing the tubes into ½-inch rings.

**Preheat the oven to 375°F.** Toss the bread crumbs with the tablespoon of olive oil and a pinch of sea salt and black pepper. Spread the bread crumbs on a rimmed baking sheet and bake until golden brown, 12 to 15 minutes.

**To serve, thread the** sliced tube pieces onto large dinner forks, and top each with a tentacle. Top each portion with a little lemon confit, some toasted bread crumbs, a few grains of sea salt, and a bit of black pepper. Garnish with the fennel fronds or chervil.

# Meyer Lemon Confit

**Makes 1 quart**

10 Meyer lemons or regular lemons

5 cups extra-virgin olive oil

4 fresh thyme sprigs

**Scrub the lemons and** slice very thin. Discard any seeds. Place the lemon slices in a saucepan with the oil and thyme sprigs and cook slowly over low heat for 30 to 35 minutes, or until the white pith has become translucent. Cool the lemon slices in the oil, then discard the thyme stems and transfer the lemon and oil to an airtight container. Tightly covered the confit will keep for up to 1 month in the refrigerator.

# Wayfare Tavern

When my business partners and I came upon an amazing piece of property for my first restaurant, the former site of Rubicon (a famed restaurant owned by Drew Nieporent and Francis Ford Coppola), we knew we wanted to do something special—something that would bring a new dimension to the San Francisco food scene. Something everyone would remember. Something nobody had tried. I did a great deal of research into the area and into what made it so unique. When all was said and done, I realized that the answer had been right there all along: Why try to come up with something new when there's a rich, unexplored history right at my fingertips?

Wayfare Tavern is my interpretation, or reimagination, if you will, of what a great San Francisco tavern might have been like at the end of the nineteenth century. The menu items are directly inspired by dishes from the late 1800s, amazing dishes that were waiting to be rediscovered, like fossils trapped in amber. Some are pretty close interpretations; others I've taken a few liberties with. Either way, they're all authentic to the time period and they're just as delicious as I imagined they would be from my research into that long-past era. It's been so gratifying to find a way to really honor the past and recognize a very important food tradition right here in my own backyard. It's food that seems at once familiar but somehow brand new at the same time. I hope you'll give these recipes a try and I look forward to you all leaving your hearts in San Francisco sometime in the near future.

# Salt-and-Pepper Chicken Wings

*with* HUMBOLDT FOG DRESSING
*and* CHILI OIL

This recipe from Wayfare Tavern in San Francisco is a simple twist on the ubiquitous Buffalo wings, a dish that has become so much a part of the American culinary vernacular that most chefs have their own variation.

**Preheat the oven to 400°F.** Toss the chicken wings with the olive oil and season liberally with salt and pepper. Spread the wings on a rimmed baking sheet and roast for 45 minutes, or until they are crispy and golden brown.

**Make the dressing:** Whisk together the sour cream, mayonnaise, lemon juice, and chives in a medium bowl. Gently stir in the crumbled cheese and season with salt and pepper.

**Arrange the wings on** a platter and drizzle with the chili oil. Scatter the radishes and celery leaves over the wings and serve with the blue cheese dressing on the side.

**Serves 4 to 6**

2 pounds chicken wings

3 tablespoons extra-virgin olive oil

Kosher salt and freshly ground black pepper

## *Humboldt Fog Dressing*

1 cup sour cream

1 cup mayonnaise

Juice of 1 lemon

2 tablespoons chopped fresh chives

1 cup crumbled Humboldt Fog or other blue cheese

Kosher salt and freshly ground black pepper

1 tablespoon Smoked Paprika Chili Oil (page 32)

½ cup thinly sliced radishes

1 handful celery leaves

# Chicken Livers

*with* CARAMELIZED ENDIVE *and* PICKLED RED ONIONS

**Chicken livers, when cooked right, have just about the sexiest texture of any food I can think of. I like to balance their rich, mineral notes with endive made sweet by caramelizing over low heat. With the pickled onions it's the perfect bite.**

**Serves 8 to 10**

1 large red onion, thinly sliced

1 cup red wine vinegar, or more as needed

1 pound fresh chicken livers, the very freshest you can find

Extra-virgin olive oil

2 shallots, thinly sliced

½ cup Cognac

Kosher salt and freshly ground black pepper

4 Belgian endives

3 tablespoons unsalted butter

5 slices sourdough bread, grilled or toasted and halved diagonally

1 cup arugula

**Place the onion slices** in a jar or small bowl and add enough vinegar to cover. Cover the container and set aside for at least 2 hours and preferably overnight to pickle the onions.

**Rinse the chicken livers** well with cold water then gently pat them dry with paper towels, removing as much moisture as possible. Heat a large skillet over medium heat until very hot. Add a 2-count of oil to the pan and when it is hot add half the chicken livers and half the shallots. (Not overcrowding the pan is the key to cooking the chicken livers properly.) Sauté for 2 minutes, then add ¼ cup of the Cognac. Carefully use a match to ignite the Cognac and let it reduce slightly, season the livers with salt and pepper, and transfer to a food processor. Return the skillet to the heat, get it hot again, and repeat with the remaining livers, shallots, and Cognac. Add the second batch of sautéed livers to the food processor and puree until smooth. Season with salt and pepper. Scrape the pâté into a bowl, place a piece of plastic wrap directly on the surface, and refrigerate until well chilled.

**Preheat the oven to 375°F.** Halve the endives lengthwise and sprinkle with salt and pepper. Heat a large skillet over high heat and, once hot, add the butter and the endives, cut side down. Sauté for 5 minutes to brown the endives, then slide the skillet into the oven. Roast for 20 minutes, or until the endives are tender and caramelized.

**To serve, smear a** nice amount of the chicken liver pâté on each piece of grilled bread. Add a few endive spears and top with a few rounds of the pickled red onion and some arugula.

# Barbecued Oysters

## with PORK BELLY *and* PICKLED SHALLOTS

When barbecue sauce is grill-roasted on an oyster, it balances out its fleshiness the way cocktail sauce does. The pork belly is the third leg of the stool, flavorwise, and the pickled shallots add a sweet acidic tang. This makes a generous amount of barbecue sauce; use leftovers on any grilled food, burgers, you name it.

**Make the sauce:** Wrap the bacon around the thyme and tie with kitchen twine. Heat a 2-count of oil in a large saucepan over medium heat. Add the thyme bundle and cook slowly for 3 or 4 minutes to render the bacon fat and give the sauce a nice smoky taste. Add the onions and garlic and cook slowly without coloring for 5 minutes. Add the remaining sauce ingredients, stir, and cook over low heat for 20 minutes. Discard the thyme bundle.

**Prepare a hot fire** in a charcoal grill or preheat your gas grill to high. In addition, set your oven to broil.

**Cut the pork belly** into 12 very thin small pieces, roughly 1 inch square. Remove the top shell from each oyster and spoon a heaping teaspoon of barbecue sauce onto each. Top with a pork belly square. Place the oysters on the grill, cover the grill, and cook over high heat for 4 to 5 minutes, or until the sauce is bubbling. Transfer the oysters to a rimmed baking sheet and slide under the broiler for 1 to 2 minutes to render the pork belly. Before serving, top with a few rounds of pickled shallot.

### Makes 1 dozen

*The Ultimate Barbecue Sauce*

1 bacon slice

1 bunch fresh thyme

Extra-virgin olive oil

½ onion, chopped

2 garlic cloves, chopped

2 cups ketchup

¼ cup packed light brown sugar

¼ cup molasses

2 tablespoons red or white wine vinegar

1 tablespoon ground mustard powder

1 teaspoon ground cumin

1 teaspoon paprika or smoked paprika (pimentón)

Freshly ground black pepper

6-ounce slab of pork belly

12 Hog Island oysters

¼ cup Pickled Shallots (page 193)

# Bone Marrow

with RUTABAGA JAM, GRILLED BREAD, *and* HERB SALAD

Bone marrow is not for everybody, but if you love it, you love it. It's almost obscenely rich. It's traditionally served with a sweet compote of some kind; I've paired it with a jam made of slowly simmered rutabaga. If you can get your butcher to split the marrow bones for you, this is actually a snap.

**Make the rutabaga jam:**
Combine the rutabaga, cider vinegar, sugar, and salt in a medium saucepan and bring to a boil over high heat. Reduce the heat to medium and simmer until the rutabaga is very soft. Transfer the mixture to a food processor and puree until smooth. (The rutabaga jam can be made ahead of time and refrigerated for a day or two.)

**Bring the vinegar to** a boil in a small saucepan. Remove from the heat and add the sliced shallots. Cool completely. Transfer the shallots and pickling liquid to a jar. Tightly covered the shallots and refrigerate; they will keep in the refrigerator for up to 1 month.

**Take the beef bones** out of the refrigerator 1 hour before cooking to allow them to come to room temperature. Preheat the broiler and adjust your oven rack to the second highest position. Stir together the panko, chopped parsley, and the tablespoon of olive oil in a small bowl.

**Arrange the beef bones,** cut side up, on a baking sheet, and broil until the marrow is translucent, 10 to 15 minutes. Sprinkle the marrow bones with the panko mixture, then return to the broiler. Broil until the bread crumbs are golden brown, about a minute or two.

**Brush the toasted bread** with a little olive oil and sprinkle with sea salt and pepper. Toss the pickled shallots with the whole-leaf parsley, chives, and tarragon. Place a marrow bone on each plate and serve with some of the rutabaga jam, toasted bread, and herb salad.

**Serves 4**

*Rutabaga Jam*

1 pound rutabaga, peeled and diced

2 cups cider vinegar

1 cup sugar

2 teaspoons kosher salt

*Pickled Shallots*

4 large shallots, thinly sliced

1½ cups red wine vinegar

4 beef bones, halved lengthwise by your butcher

2 cups panko bread crumbs

1 tablespoon chopped fresh flat-leaf parsley plus 1 cup whole flat-leaf parsley leaves

1 tablespoon extra-virgin olive oil, plus more for the bread

4 slices rustic country bread, grilled or toasted

Coarse sea salt and freshly ground black pepper

½ cup 1-inch-long pieces of chives

2 tablespoons fresh tarragon leaves

# Potato, Leek, and Sorrel Soup

## with CRÈME FRAÎCHE *and* MUSTARD FLOWERS

I made this soup out on the Dierks Farm in Bolinas, taking whatever was fresh from the farm and cooking it over an outdoor fire. For something that was conceived on the fly, it turned out to be pretty amazing, and now it's a mainstay on our menus.

**Place a heavy-bottomed** soup pot over medium heat and add a 3-count of oil. Add the yellow onions and garlic and cook until translucent, about 10 minutes. Add the potatoes, spring onions, broth, and salt. Bring to a simmer, then reduce the heat to low, cover, and cook for 45 minutes, or until the potatoes fall apart.

**Using a ladle, transfer** about half of the soup to a blender and blend until smooth. (Never fill the blender more than half way when blending hot liquids, as the steam can build up and force the top of the blender to come off; you may need to do this in batches.) Return the pureed soup to the soup pot and swirl to combine with the unblended portion. Fold in the sorrel. The soup will be creamy but slightly rustic and chunky. Ladle into bowls and garnish with freshly cracked black pepper, and with smoked olive oil, a dollop of crème fraîche, and some edible flowers, if you have them.

**Serves 6 to 8**

Extra-virgin olive oil

1 large yellow onion, diced

3 garlic cloves, peeled and smashed with the side of a chef's knife

2 pounds Yukon Gold potatoes, quartered

1 bunch spring onions, sliced ½ inch thick

2 quarts low-sodium chicken or vegetable broth

2 tablespoons kosher salt

4 cups sorrel, cut crosswise into ½-inch strips

Freshly cracked black pepper

Smoked olive oil (optional)

Crème fraîche (optional)

Edible flowers, such as mustard flowers (optional)

# Apple Parsnip Soup

## with ANGELS on HORSEBACK

If you've never cooked with parsnips, don't wait another minute; they are amazing. Try them roasted, sautéed, as a substitute for mashed potatoes—or in this recipe, a perfect autumn soup that's so delicious you'll want to lick the bowl clean. Add oysters and bacon and what's not to love?

**Melt the butter in** a heavy-bottomed soup pot over medium heat. Add the onions and cook without letting them brown until they are soft and translucent, about 10 minutes. Add the parsnips and cook for another 15 minutes, stirring occasionally to prevent scorching. Add the apples and cook for another 10 minutes; the apple-parsnip mixture should resemble a compote at this point. Set aside 1 cup of the apple-parsnip mixture then add the broth and 2 tablespoons salt. Bring the soup to a boil, then reduce the heat to a simmer, add the cream, and cook until the parsnips are very soft. Puree the soup in a blender, working in batches, until smooth and creamy. (Be careful not to overfill the blender as the hot soup will expand as you puree it.)

**Heat 3 inches of** vegetable oil in a deep saucepan to 350°F over medium-high heat, Cut the bacon slices in half crosswise, then wrap each oyster in a bacon strip, pressing the ends to secure. Roll the wrapped oysters in the cornmeal. Carefully lower the oysters into the hot oil and fry until they are golden brown, about 2 minutes. Drain on paper towels and immediately sprinkle with salt and pepper.

**To serve, mound a** heaping tablespoon of the reserved apple-parsnip mixture in the middle of each shallow soup bowl, and top with a fried oyster. Carefully pour more soup around the oyster, and garnish with thyme leaves and a drizzle of smoked olive oil.

### Serve 8 to 10

3 tablespoons unsalted butter

1 large yellow onion, coarsely chopped

3 pounds parsnips, peeled and coarsely chopped

2 green apples, peeled, cored, and coarsely chopped

3 Pink Lady apples or Golden Delicious apples, peeled, cored, and coarsely chopped

3 quarts low-sodium chicken or vegetable broth

Kosher salt

2 cups heavy cream

Vegetable oil, for deep-frying

4 thick-cut bacon slices

8 small or medium fresh oysters, shucked

2 cups cornmeal

Freshly ground black pepper

Smoked olive oil, for garnish

# Roasted Beet Salad

*with* MARCONA ALMONDS, WHIPPED GOAT CHEESE, *and* MAPLE BALSAMIC DRESSING

I love beets. Their "dirty" sweet, earthy flavor always triggers something primal, making me think of early man, roasting gathered roots in the embers of a tribal fire. This recipe combines roasted and raw beets with lots of well-rounded high and low notes.

**Make the dressing:** Combine the shallots, balsamic vinegar, olive oil, and maple syrup in a small jar with a tight-fitting lid. Season with salt and pepper. Shake until well mixed.

**Preheat the oven to 400°F.** Wash the beets well and trim the root end. Cut two 12-inch sheets of aluminum foil. Lay one piece of foil on your work surface and put the beets in the center. Drizzle with a 3-count of olive oil and sprinkle with the thyme, salt, and pepper. Cover with the second piece of foil and crimp the edges several times to make a pouch. Place the pouch on a baking sheet and roast the beets for about 1 hour or until a knife pierces a beet smoothly. (You can stick the knife right through the foil.) Take the pouch out of the oven, open it up to let the beets cool, and then peel the beets and cut each into 4 wedges.

**Place the goat cheese** in a mixing bowl and drizzle with 2 tablespoons of olive oil. Beat vigorously with a whisk until the oil and goat cheese are combined and fluffy. Season with salt and pepper.

**To assemble the salads,** dollop the goat cheese mixture onto a serving plate. Scatter the beets and almonds over the goat cheese and drizzle with vinaigrette. Top with the arugula.

**Serves 4**

### Maple Balsamic Dressing

1 shallot, finely minced

3 tablespoons balsamic vinegar

½ cup olive oil

2 tablespoons pure maple syrup

Kosher salt and freshly ground black pepper

---

1½ pounds baby beets, preferably a mix of red and yellow

Extra-virgin olive oil

1 teaspoon fresh thyme leaves

Kosher salt and freshly ground black pepper

4 ounces fresh goat cheese

½ cup Marcona almonds

¼ cup micro arugula or pea sprouts

# Frisée Salad

## *with* EGG *and* BACON

Frisée aux lardons is a tried-and-true French bistro classic and in the cooler months of the year I grab it any time I see it on a menu. If you've never made it at home you're missing out; it's so easy to make and can be substantial enough to be a meal on its own.

**Make the vinaigrette:** Combine the minced shallots, mustards, oil, vinegar, honey, salt, and pepper in a jar with a tight-fitting lid. Shake for 20 seconds or until everything is emulsified. (Leftover dressing will keep in the refrigerator for up to 2 weeks.)

**Place the bacon in** a cold skillet and place the pan over medium heat. Slowly render the bacon until it is crisp, 12 to 15 minutes. Remove the bacon from the pan with a slotted spoon and drain on paper towels.

**Place the eggs in** a saucepan with cold water to cover. Bring to a boil over high heat, then immediately remove from the heat, cover the pan, and let the eggs stand in the hot water for exactly 14 minutes. Drain the eggs and cover with cold water. Once cool, peel the eggs and halve lenthwise.

**Place the frisée in** a big salad bowl and add the bacon and pickled shallots. Add the vinaigrette and toss to coat the greens. Arrange the hard-boiled eggs on top.

**Serves 4 to 6**

### *Vinaigrette*

1 small shallot, finely minced

1 teaspoon Dijon mustard

1 teaspoon whole-grain mustard

½ cup extra-virgin olive oil

¼ cup sherry vinegar

1 tablespoon honey

½ teaspoon kosher salt

¼ teaspoon freshly ground black pepper

3 large heads or 5 small heads of frisee, washed and dried

10 thick-cut bacon slices, diced

6 eggs

# My Winemaking Family

Napa Valley is just up the road from my Mill Valley home, but in many respects it is light years away. California's wine country is one of the most idyllic places anywhere in the world, and if my new Nor Cal life is TF 2.0, then retiring to Napa is probably TF 3.0 . . . or maybe 3.5.

Much like the city of San Francisco, her neighbor just an hour's drive to the north, the Napa Valley has a history that is often overlooked and underappreciated. Called Napa, meaning "land of plenty," by the native Wappo Indians, the valley was once a wild frontier with an abundance of grizzly bears, salmon, elk, and mountain lions. But while the region changed over time, the modern era arguably began with the first homesteader, George Calvert Yount, who put down roots in 1836 in what is now know as Yountville, home to Thomas Keller's venerable French Laundry and Michael Chiarello's Bottega, among other important dining institutions.

Charles Krug is widely acknowleged as having founded the very first commercial winery in Napa in 1861, spawning several hundred imitators in the following decades. But in the latter part of the nineteenth century, an aphid-like pest called phylloxera wiped out most of the valley's vines and effectively reset the region's winemaking capabilities. In 1919, Prohibition dealt an even greater blow to the wineries, and only a few survived by continuing to grow grapes for wine under religious auspices. While the business of wine may have been crippled, the spirit of the Napa Valley lived on; and upon the repeal of Prohibition in 1933, winemakers regrouped with a deep sense of camaraderie, a commitment to the noble virtues of the grape, and, of course, a shared love of great food. California was back on the map and on its way to becoming a world-class winemaking destination.

In 1936, an Italian immigrant and enterprising fruit wholesaler named Cesare Mondavi purchased a stake in the Sunny St. Helena winery, where his first son, Robert, would become involved in the daily operations. In 1943, Cesare, with sons Robert and Peter, purchased the Charles Krug winery to further the family's stake in the wine game, and since then the Mondavi family name has been virtually synonymous with the Napa Valley. In truth, without Robert Mondavi's entrepreneurial spirit, passion for the promotion of California as one of the world's great winemaking regions, and

undying love of both the business and art of wine-making, one of California's greatest exports may never have been.

Of course, it's no secret that the symbiotic relationship between food and wine has inspired generations of chefs and diners the world over. I've been capitivated by wine from my first sips at the dinner table on through my sojourns to the historic grape-growing regions of France and Italy, and for me, winemaking has always been on the agenda. Living in California has made that possibility a reality.

There's something about the process of making wine that is mysterious in a really sexy way, and I'll admit, I'm hooked. For the past three years, I've been making single-barrel vintages of zinfandel and pinot noir and a bit to my own pleasant surprise, my first vintage, TF Zin 06, received a score of 92 from *Wine Spectator*; it was beyond my wildest dreams to hit the cover off of the ball on my first try. Recently, my friend Dina Mondavi, granddaughter of the late Robert, suggested getting together with her family to see if there was a way to work together. That first friendly meeting has changed the game for me. I am both humbled and proud to be welcomed into the Mondavi's winemaking family.

Together, this year the Mondavis and I will launch a new line of wines to be selectively distributed around the world. In partnership with Michael (son of Robert) and his children Rob and Dina, my personal winemaking style is being further refined as we move from limited-scale production to working with the vast resources of the Mondavi family, adding gorgeous sauvignon blancs and cabernet sauvignons to my zinfandels and pinot noirs.

As a team, we spend a lot of time together tasting wines, and oftentimes it really just feels right to enjoy the pleasures of our business over a meal. Recently, I shared my new winemaking family with my father, Winston, and it was a very memorable experience to discuss wine and lay out multiple generations of knowledge and opinions.

Yes, I realize how fortunate I am to be able to combine my business with pleasure . . . time and time again. Great food, like great wine, is simultaneously subjective and universal. Both generate spirited discussion and, in the right company, a convivial spirit that literally breathes life into those lucky enough to share the table with one another.

# Mains
# & Sides

# Seared Halibut

*with* BROCCOLI PUREE *and* RED-EYE GRAVY

This is a great show-off dish that doesn't require very much effort at all. I think the contrast of the hot fish with the cool broccoli puree is fantastic, but you can warm the puree in the microwave if you prefer.

**Serves 4**

1 head broccoli

1 cup plain yogurt

1 cup sour cream

Grated zest and juice of 1 lemon

Kosher salt and freshly ground black pepper

4 thin slices pancetta

1 cup coffee

Extra-virgin olive oil

4 skinless halibut fillets, 4 to 5 ounces each

1 tablespoon unsalted butter

8 fresh thyme sprigs

2 tablespoons capers, drained

**Bring a large pot** of salted water to a boil and fill a large bowl with ice water. Cut the broccoli into small florets and slice the stems very thin. Blanch the broccoli in the boiling water for 30 seconds, then drain and plunge in the ice water. Once cool, drain the broccoli and transfer to a blender or food processor. Add the yogurt, sour cream, lemon zest and juice, and salt and pepper. Blend until smooth and refrigerate to preserve the broccoli's bright green color.

**Place a skillet over** medium heat and add the pancetta slices. Cook until crisp, then drain the pancetta on paper towels, leaving the rendered fat in the skillet. To make the red-eye gravy, whisk the coffee into the pancetta fat and cook over medium-high heat for 5 to 7 minutes to reduce slightly, then season with salt and pepper. Set aside and keep warm.

**Preheat the oven to 400°F.** Place a large ovenproof skillet over high heat. Once hot add a 2-count of olive oil. Season the fish on both sides with salt and pepper, and place in the hot pan. Cook without moving the fillets for 3 to 4 minutes, or until a nice brown crust begins to develop. Turn the fish seared side up, add the butter and thyme to the pan, and transfer the skillet to the oven. Roast for 6 to 8 minutes, until the fish is firm and starting to flake around the sides. Transfer the fillets to a warm plate, seared side up, and keep warm.

**Heat a 2-count of** extra-virgin olive oil in a small skillet or saucepan. Once the oil starts to shimmer, add the capers and fry until crispy, about 2 minutes. Use a slotted spoon to transfer the crispy capers to paper towels to drain.

**Spoon a nice big** dollop of the chilled broccoli puree onto the center of each plate. Place a halibut fillet on top, seared side up, and add a piece of pancetta, a thyme sprig, and some fried capers to each plate. Reheat the red-eye gravy if necessary and spoon a few tablespoons around the broccoli puree.

# Seared Salmon

*with* MUSTARD-BRAISED BRUSSELS SPROUTS

Pairing meat sauces with fish is something that I've been doing for more than a decade; it gives these dishes a depth and hearty structure that is especially welcome in the winter months. Serve this with a great pinot noir.

**Serves 4**

1 pound Brussels sprouts, halved

4 tablespoons (½ stick) unsalted buttor

1 large yellow onion, diced

2 garlic cloves, peeled and smashed with the side of a chef's knife

1 quart heavy cream

6 fresh lemon thyme sprigs

2 tablespoons yellow mustard

2 tablespoons whole-grain mustard

12 ounces skinless wild salmon fillet, cut crosswise into 8 narrow strips

Extra-virgin olive oil

Kosher salt and freshly ground black pepper

4 very thin slices pancetta

¼ cup store-bought veal of beef demi-glace

Handful of gourmet potato chips, for garnish

Thyme leaves, for garnish

**Bring a large saucepan** of salted water to a boil and place a large bowl of ice water next to the stove. Add the Brussels sprouts to the boiling water and cook for 1 minute. Immediately drain the sprouts and plunge them into the ice water to stop the cooking process. Drain and set aside.

**Return the pot to** the stove over medium heat and add 3 tablespoons of the butter. Once melted, add the onions and garlic and cook until the onions are translucent, about 10 minutes. Add the cream, lemon thyme sprigs, and both mustards, and cook over medium heat until reduced by a third, about 20 minutes. Fold in the drained Brussels sprouts.

**Preheat the oven to 450°F.**
Working with two of the salmon strips at a time, nestle the fish into a yin-yang shape and secure with kitchen string. Place an ovenproof skillet over high heat. Once it is hot, add a 2-count of extra-virgin olive oil. Season the fish on both sides with salt and pepper. Gently lay the 4 salmon rolls in the pan and sear until golden brown on one side, about 3 minutes. Add the remaining tablespoon of butter to the pan, turn the fillets over, and transfer the skillet to the oven. Roast for 10 to 12 minutes, or until the salmon is nearly cooked through; it should be slightly pink in the center. Remove the string.

**In a small skillet,** cook the pancetta slices over low heat until the fat is rendered and the pancetta is crisp. Drain the pancetta on paper towels. In a small saucepan, bring the demi-glace just to a simmer over medium heat; immediately remove from the heat. Spoon some of the Brussels sprouts onto each plate and top with the salmon, crispy pancetta, and a few potato chips. Drizzle the veal jus around the plate and sprinkle with a few lemon thyme leaves.

# Petrale Sole

_with_ SAUCE BONNE FEMME

As I was writing the menu for Wayfare Tavern, I needed some historical dishes to support my concept of an old American tavern that might have been there since the late 1890s. That search led me to Sole Bonne Femme, a dish that was served at San Francisco's grand Palace Hotel built in 1875. I've put a modern stamp on the dish but at its heart this version is classic and true.

**Serves 8**

4 tablespoons (½ stick) unsalted butter

1 shallot, minced

2 cups dry white wine

2 quarts Fish Stock (page 216)

2 cups heavy cream

Kosher salt

Ground white pepper

8 petrale sole or flounder fillets, about 6 ounces each

2 tablespoons fresh thyme leaves

Extra-virgin olive oil

16 large white mushrooms

2 tablespoons finely slivered fresh sage leaves

**Place a deep skillet** over medium heat and add 1 tablespoon of the butter. When the butter has melted, add the minced shallots and cook until translucent, 2 to 3 minutes. Add the wine, turn the heat to high, and cook until the wine has reduced by half, 10 to 15 minutes. Add the fish stock and simmer for 20 minutes. Stir in the cream and 2 more tablespoons of the butter; season with salt and white pepper.

**Season the fish fillets** on both sides with salt and white pepper and sprinkle the second side with the thyme leaves. Roll the fillets tightly, enclosing the thyme leaves, and use a toothpick to secure each roll. Gently slip the fish rolls into the liquid, making sure they are submerged. Cook over low heat with the liquid at a bare simmer, for 20 to 25 minutes, or until the fish is cooked through but not falling apart.

**While the fish cooks,** set another skillet over high heat and add a 2-count of olive oil. Once hot, add the mushrooms and cook, stirring, for 5 minutes, then add the remaining 1 tablespoon of butter. The mushrooms should have a nice golden color.

**Use a slotted spoon** to transfer each fish roll to a plate or shallow bowl. Remove the toothpicks. Spoon a few tablespoons of the poaching liquid over each serving and top with the sautéed mushrooms and sage.

# Fish Stock

### Makes 2 quarts

3 pounds fish bones from nonoily fish such as flounder, sole, or cod

1 yellow onion, halved

1 leek, trimmed, cut into large pieces, and washed well

3 celery stalks, cut into large pieces

1 small fresh red chile

1 big strip orange zest

1 big strip lemon zest

1 bunch fresh thyme

4 bay leaves

1 teaspoon black peppercorns

1 cup dry white wine

**Rinse the fish bones** very well until there is absolutely no blood remaining. Place them in a large stockpot and add the remaining stock ingredients. Pour in only enough cold water to cover the bones and vegetables, about 2 quarts. Bring to a boil, then immediately reduce the heat to low and simmer for 20 minutes. As the stock cooks, skim any foam and impurities that rise to the surface; add a little more water if necessary to keep the bones covered.

**Strain the stock through** a fine-mesh sieve into another pot and discard the bones and vegetable solids. Use the stock immediately or, if you plan on storing it, cool the stock, transfer to a storage containers, and refrigerate for a day or two, or freeze for up to 3 months.

# Roasted Chicken

*with* SALSA VERDE *and* FRENCH FRIES

Jonathan Waxman is a California-trained chef who made his name in New York City with West Coast–inflected fare at restaurants like Jams and now Barbuto. His roasted chicken sets the bar for any chef. Here I've brought it full circle back to its California roots.

**Preheat the oven to 375°F.** Place a large cast iron skillet over high heat for 5 minutes, or until the pan is good and hot. Pat the chicken halves dry with a paper towel, then rub all over with 3 tablespoons of olive oil and sprinkle generously with salt and pepper. Carefully place the chicken halves in the pan, skin side down. (If your pan is not large, sear the halves one at a time.) Sear until the skin is golden brown, then slide the skillet into the oven.

**Roast the chicken halves** for 40 minutes, or until the juices run clear when the thigh is pierced. Transfer the chicken to a platter to rest skin side up for 15 minutes reducing the oven temperature to 250°F.

**When the chicken goes** into the oven, peel the potatoes and cut lengthwise into ⅓-inch slices. Stack the slices and cut lengthwise into ⅓-inch fries. Place the fries in a large bowl with cold water to cover and soak for 20 minutes. Drain the water, refill, and soak for another 20 minutes. Drain the potatoes and pat as dry as possible.

**Heat the vegetable oil in deep** fryer or large, heavy-bottomed pot to 375°F. Working in small batches, fry the potatoes for 8 to 10 minutes, or until golden brown and tender. Transfer to a paper-towel-lined baking sheet and keep warm in the oven while you fry the remaining potatoes.

**Make the salsa verde:** Place the parsley, thyme, tarragon, olives, capers, and anchovies on a cutting board. Chop them with a knife until they are very fine. Transfer to a bowl and stir in the lemon zest, olive oil, and vinegar. Season to taste with salt and pepper.

**To serve, toss the** arugula with a squirt of lemon juice and a quick glug of olive oil. Arrange the chicken halves on 2 plates with a pile of the arugula. Spoon some of the salsa verde over the chicken and serve with the fries.

## Serves 2

1 whole chicken, split (3 to 4 pounds)

Extra-virgin olive oil

Kosher salt and freshly ground black pepper

6 large russet potatoes

2 quarts vegetable oil, for deep-frying

## Salsa Verde

¼ cup fresh flat-leaf parsley leaves

1 tablespoon fresh thyme leaves

1 tablespoon fresh tarragon leaves

¼ cup pitted green olives

2 tablespoons drained capers

3 anchovy fillets

1 teaspoon grated lemon zest, preferably from a Meyer lemon

½ cup extra-virgin olive oil

1 tablespoon red wine vinegar

Kosher salt and freshly ground black pepper

2 cups arugula

½ lemon, preferably a Meyer lemon

# Roasted Pheasant

*with* BRIOCHE, TRUFFLE, PORK, *and* FOIE GRAS STUFFING

You don't see pheasant on restaurant menus very often these days, but at one time it was considered the height of elegance and every fine restaurant had its own preparation. I think it's due for a revival, because the rich, lean meat pairs perfectly with some of my favorite foods: foie gras, truffles, and bacon. You could make this with chickens or even a turkey, but if you have a source for pheasant, give it a try. The stuffing is really beyond.

**Make the stuffing: Place** the bread cubes in a mixing bowl and pour the milk over them, stirring to combine. Set aside.

**Melt the butter in** a skillet over medium heat. Add the carrots, celery, onions, leeks, fennel, and garlic, and cook, stirring, for 10 minutes, or until the carrots are beginning to soften and the onions are translucent. Remove from the heat and set aside to cool.

**Place the pork in** a large mixing bowl and add the cooled vegetables. Drain the brioche and gently squeeze out the excess milk. Add the bread to the bowl along with the pistachios, thyme, foie gras, truffle, and Cognac and mix gently. Season with salt and pepper.

**Preheat the oven to 375°F.** Rinse the birds inside and out with cool water and pat dry. Place the pheasants on your cutting board breast side down and use kitchen shears to cut all the way along each side of the backbone, freeing it completely. Discard the backbones and open up the birds, then grasp the breastbone with your fingers and gently pull it away from the breast

*(continued on page 222)*

## Serves 4 to 6

### Stuffing

6 thick slices brioche loaf, cut into large cubes

2 cups whole milk

½ cup (1 stick) unsalted butter

2 carrots, finely diced

4 celery stalks, finely diced

1 large yellow onion, finely diced

1 leek, halved, sliced crosswise, and washed well, finely diced

½ fennel bulb, finely diced

3 garlic cloves, minced

1 pound ground pork

1 cup pistachios, crushed

2 tablespoons fresh thyme leaves

⅓ lobe (about 6 ounces) foie gras, cut into large cubes

½ fresh black truffle, shaved, or 2 tablespoons truffle oil

2 tablespoons Cognac

Kosher salt and freshly ground black pepper

2 fresh pheasants or chickens

2 thick-cut bacon slices

Extra-virgin olive oil

Kosher salt and freshly ground black pepper

meat; discard the breastbones. (You can also ask your butcher to "spatchcock" the pheasants for you if you prefer.)

**Fill each bird loosely** with stuffing. Reshape the bird around the stuffing and top with a strip of bacon. Use kitchen string to tie it in a neat bundle. Rub the birds all over with olive oil, season with salt and pepper, and place in a large roasting pan.

**Roast uncovered for** 1 hour, or until the internal temperature of the meat (not the stuffing) registers 160°F. Let the birds rest for 15 minutes before serving halved or sliced crosswise.

# The Pheasant Hunt

As a chef, I think it's important to know where your food comes from. And for a carnivore, let alone a locavore, the experience of taking an animal from its habitat to the table is true culinary immersion. With that in mind, I ventured out with some friends and family for a day of pheasant hunting a short distance to the north in Petaluma.

Local pheasant is one of those special items that I felt might work very well at El Paseo and I wanted to experience the process from start to finish, from field to table. Back in 1964, Mike Sustos, a native San Franciscan who had returned to the Bay Area after fighting in the Pacific with the First Marine Division, started Black Point Sporting Club, which would become what is now one of the oldest upland hunting clubs in California. Mike and his wife, Maria, raised their family on the property, and since Mike's passing, Maria has kept Black Point up and running for hunters year after year. With his mother, Mike Junior now runs the operation with meticulous care for the legacy his father created and with deep dedication to sportsmanship and environmental concerns. Mike Junior and his talented dog, Dottie, walked the fields with us and we harvested several beautiful ringneck pheasants for the evening supper. It's roots to the core and I appreciate the Sustos family's efforts to provide this experience.

# Porkie Pie

In the United Kingdom, a "porkie pie" is Cockney rhyming slang for a big fat lie, but believe me when I tell you this is an amazing dish.

**Make the pastry dough:** Sift the flour and salt into a mixing bowl. Using your fingertips or a pastry blender, work in the butter until the mixture looks like coarse bread crumbs. Slowly add 4 tablespoons ice water, a tablespoon at a time, and mix with a fork until the dough just comes together when squeezed with your fingers. If the dough is still dry at this point, add another tablespoon of ice water. Knead the dough until it is smooth, about 5 more minutes. Once smooth, divide the dough in half, with one piece being slightly larger for the bottom piece, and shape into disks. Wrap the dough disks in plastic wrap, refrigerate, and let them rest for at least 2 hours, and ideally, overnight. (Dough that is not allowed to rest will shrink when baked.)

**Combine the carrots,** celery, onions and garlic in a food processor, and pulse until coarsely chopped, 12 to 15 pulses. Place a large pot on the stove over high heat. Once the pot is hot, add a 4-count of olive oil. In a large mixing bowl, combine the pork with the chopped vegetables and mix well. Add this mixture to the hot pan, and sauté for 10 to 15 minutes, or until the pork gets browned and the vegetables have released most of their moisture. Add the tomato paste, canned tomatoes, thyme, and wine.

Cook for 20 minutes. Use a ladle to dip out 2 cups of the liquid from the pot and set aside for the sauce. Continue to cook the ragù until the remaining liquid has almost entirely cooked off, another 20 minutes. Season with salt and pepper and set aside to cool.

**Preheat the oven to 375°F.** Roll the larger disk of pastry dough into a round large enough to fit a 9-inch pie pan. Fit the dough into the pan and fill with the cooled pork ragù. Roll out the second dough disk and place over the filling. Pinch the edges together all the way around and poke a hole in the top for steam to escape. Use a pastry brush to brush the entire crust with the beaten egg. Bake the pie until golden brown, 50 to 60 minutes. Remove from the oven and let cool for at least 15 minutes.

**While the pie bakes,** melt 4 tablespoons of the butter in a skillet over medium heat. Whisk in the flour and cook over medium-low heat without browning for 10 minutes to cook out the raw flour taste. Whisk in the reserved cooking liquid and simmer for 20 minutes, then add the remaining 2 tablespoons butter, salt and pepper. Whisk to incorporate. Keep warm.

**Serve the porkie pie** warm with the warm sauce.

## Serves 6 to 8

### Pastry Dough

2½ cups all-purpose flour

1 teaspoon kosher salt

1 cup plus 4 tablespoons (2½ sticks) chilled butter, cut into pieces

4 to 5 tablespoons ice water

2 large carrots, peeled and coarsely chopped

2 celery stalks, coarsely chopped

1 large yellow onion, coarsely chopped

3 garlic cloves, peeled

Extra-virgin olive oil

2 pounds ground pork shoulder

2 tablespoons tomato paste

1 (16-ounce) can San Marzano tomatoes, with their juices

Leaves from 1 bunch fresh thyme

4 cups dry red wine

Kosher salt and freshly ground black pepper

1 egg, lightly beaten

6 tablespoons (¾ stick) unsalted butter

¼ cup all-purpose flour

# Slow-Roasted Pork Shoulder

with ROASTED BEETS, *and* MUSTARD DRIPPINGS

I love the balance of texture and flavors in this simply prepared dish. Rolling and tying the tender meat enables you to cut it in neat slices. Serve this over Cauliflower Ricotta Pudding.

**Serves 6 to 8**

¼ cup fennel seeds

4- to 5-pound boneless pork shoulder, skin on

12 garlic cloves, minced

1 tablespoon chopped fresh thyme

1 tablespoon chopped fresh oregano

Kosher salt and freshly ground black pepper

Extra-virgin olive oil

1 bunch red baby beets (about 1½ pounds)

1 bunch yellow beets (about 1½ pounds)

1 tablespoon Dijon mustard

2 tablespoons whole-grain mustard

Cauliflower Ricotta Pudding (page 255)

Toasted bread crumbs

**Preheat the oven to 325°F.** In a small, dry skillet, toast the fennel seeds over medium heat until fragrant and golden, about 5 minutes. Transfer to a spice grinder or use a mortar and pestle to grind to a powder.

**Place the pork shoulder** on a cutting board and butterfly it, opening it up like a book to make one large flat piece. Generously rub the inside with the toasted fennel seeds, garlic, thyme, oregano, and salt and pepper. Roll up the meat like a jelly roll and use kitchen string to tie the roll every 2 inches. Rub the exterior of the roll liberally with olive oil, and season with salt and pepper.

**Place a large roasting** pan on the stovetop and get it good and hot over high heat. Add a 2-count of olive oil and sear the entire outside of the rolled shoulder until it's golden brown, about 10 minutes. Slide the pan into the oven and roast the pork until the internal temperature reaches 145°F, about 2 hours.

**Place the beets** on large squares of aluminum foil in groups of 2 or 3 and season them with oil, salt, and pepper. Wrap the beets tightly in the foil and roast along with the pork until they are tender when pierced with a fork, about 1 hour and 15 minutes.

**When the pork is** done, transfer it to a cutting board for at least 30 minutes. Pour the drippings from the roasting pan into a small skillet. Whisk in the mustards and heat gently, seasoning with salt and pepper to taste. Peel the beets and cut into quarters.

**To serve, slice the** pork about ½ inch thick. Arrange on a platter atop a bed of the cauliflower pudding and drizzle the pork with the mustard drippings. Add the beets to the platter and sprinkle bread crumbs over all.

# Veal Oscar

This classic dish was created to commemorate the 25th anniversary of King Oscar II of Sweden's ascension to the throne. The original dish featured a slice of fried veal fillet, with lobster, truffle, and two asparagus spears forming a Roman number two. I've substituted crab for the lobster, but either is amazing.

**Serves 4**

8 asparagus spears, preferably jumbo, bottom 2 inches removed

4 veal cutlets, about 3 ounces each

1 cup all-purpose flour

Kosher salt and freshly ground black pepper

4 tablespoons (½ stick) unsalted butter

1 shallot, finely chopped

1 pound fresh lump crabmeat

Béarnaise Sauce (page 236)

Fesh tarragon leaves

**Bring a pot of** salted water to a boil and fill a large bowl with ice water. Drop the asparagus into the boiling water and cook for 2 minutes, or until al dente. Remove and plunge into the ice water to stop the cooking process. Once cool, drain and set aside.

**Place each veal cutlet** between 2 pieces of plastic wrap and use the smooth side of a meat mallet or a rolling pin to pound to an even ¼-inch thickness. Cut each in half lengthwise. Place an asparagus spear on each piece of veal and roll into a cigar.

**Place the flour in** a shallow dish and season with salt and pepper. Dredge the veal rolls all over in the flour, shaking off the excess.

**Heat 2 tablespoons of** the butter in a skillet over medium-high heat. Add 4 of the veal rolls and cook until the veal is golden brown on all sides, 12 to 14 minutes. Transfer to a plate and repeat with the remaining butter and veal rolls. Arrange the veal rolls on a warm platter and keep warm. In the same pan, with the browned butter, sauté the shallots until translucent, 3 to 4 minutes. Add the crabmeat and continue to cook over high heat until crispy, about 5 minutes, stirring only once or twice to keep the pieces whole and get them nicely caramelized.

**To serve, spoon the** béarnaise sauce over the veal rolls, top with the crispy fried crab, and sprinkle with the tarragon.

# Béarnaise Sauce

### Makes 1½ cups

¼ cup chopped fresh tarragon leaves

2 shallots, minced

¼ cup champagne vinegar

¼ cup dry white wine

3 egg yolks

½ cup (1 stick) unsalted butter, melted

Kosher salt and freshly ground
black pepper

**In a small saucepan,** combine the tarragon, shallots, vinegar, and wine. Bring to a simmer over medium-high heat and cook until reduced by half, about 10 minutes. Remove from the heat and set aside.

**Set a stainless steel** bowl over a saucepan of simmering water, or use a double boiler. Add the egg yolks and whisk until doubled in volume. Slowly add the melted butter, beating constantly to prevent the eggs from scrambling, until the sauce is thickened, 10 to 12 minutes. Stir in the shallot mixture and season with salt and pepper. Keep warm until ready to serve.

# California Osso Buco

## with KUMQUAT CRANBERRY GREMOLATA

**Osso buco is the Cadillac of braised dishes, and this is my take on the Italian classic, using California zinfandel instead of the traditional Brunello.**

**Put the flour on** a large plate and season it with a fair amount of salt and pepper. Dredge the veal shanks in the seasoned flour and then tap off the excess. Heat a large, heavy pot over medium heat and hit it with a 3-count of oil. Add the butter and swirl it around the pan to melt. Add the veal shanks and sear on all sides, turning carefully with tongs, until they are a rich brown all over. Drizzle a little more oil into the pan if needed. Remove the browned veal shanks to a plate.

**Preheat the oven to 375°F.**

**Add the onions,** celery, carrots, lemon zest, garlic, bay leaves, and parsley to the same pot and cook over medium heat, scraping up the browned bits from the bottom of the pan. Cook the vegetables until they start to get some color and develop a deep, rich aroma, about 15 minutes. Season with salt and pepper. Nestle the veal shanks back into the pot, add the wine, and bring

to a boil. Reduce the heat and simmer for 20 minutes, or until reduced by half. Add the beef broth and tomatoes, crushing them with your hands as they go in the pot, and stir everything together. Cover the pot, transfer it to the oven, and braise the veal for 2 hours, removing the lid after 1½ hours. The sauce should be thick and the veal tender and nearly falling off the bone. Discard the bay leaves.

**Make the gremolata:** Toast the pine nuts in a small, dry skillet over medium-low heat, shaking the pan often, until fragrant and golden, 6 to 8 minutes. Cool the pine nuts, then finely chop and place in a mixing bowl. Fold in the kumquats, cranberries, garlic, and parsley.

**Serve the osso buco** in shallow bowls sprinkled with some of the gremolata.

**Serves 4**

1 cup all-purpose flour

Kosher salt and freshly ground black pepper

4 (2-inch) pieces veal shank

Extra-virgin olive oil

3 tablespoons unsalted butter

1 onion, diced

1 celery stalk, diced

2 carrots, peeled and diced

Zest of 1 lemon, peeled off in fat strips with a vegetable peeler

6 garlic cloves, peeled and smashed

2 bay leaves

¼ cup chopped fresh flat-leaf parsley

1 bottle California zinfandel

2 cups low-sodium beef broth

1 (28-ounce) can whole San Marzano tomatoes, drained

### Kumquat Cranberry Gremolata

¼ cup pine nuts

1 cup sliced kumquats

¼ cup chopped dried cranberries

2 garlic cloves, minced

2 tablespoons chopped fresh flat-leaf parsley

# Lamb Shank

BRAISED IN STOUT GRAVY *with* WATERCRESS SALAD

Stout creates a beautiful syrupy glaze that blends so well with meat juices. Now when the temperatures dip, when I'm cooking anything north of a chicken on the food chain I ask myself, "What would a stout glaze taste like on that?"

**Preheat the oven to 325°F.**
Combine the coriander seeds, fennel seeds, and peppercorns in a small, heavy skillet. Toast over medium-high heat until the seeds are aromatic and slightly darker, about 2 minutes. Transfer to a spice grinder or use a mortar and pestle to grind to a fine powder. Rub each shank with a generous teaspoon of the spice blend and sprinkle with salt.

**Heat a 4-count of** oil in a large, wide, heavy pot over high heat. Add the shanks and brown on all sides, turning often, about 15 minutes. Remove the shanks from the pan. Add a 2-count of oil to the same pot, then add the onions, celery, carrots, leeks, garlic, and bay leaves. Sauté over high heat until the vegetables start to soften and take on some color, about 15 minutes. Add the tomatoes, (crushing them by hand), tomato paste, and red wine. Stir to combine and cook for an additional 10 minutes

over high heat. Add the beef broth and Guinness, then return the seared lamb shanks to the pot, nestling them into the liquid. Bring the braising liquid to a simmer, then cover the pot and slide it into the oven.

**Braise the shanks for** 2½ hours total, adding the thyme and marjoram to the pot after 2 hours. The lamb should be tender and falling away from the bone.

**While the shanks braise,** place the carrots on a baking sheet. Drizzle with a little olive oil and season with salt and pepper. Roast for 20 to 25 minutes, or until nearly tender.

**Transfer the shanks to** a plate, then strain the braising liquid through a fine-mesh sieve. Return the sauce and shanks to the pot to combine. Toss the watercress with the lemon juice and serve with the shanks, spooning plenty of the stout gravy on top.

## Serves 4

2 tablespoons coriander seeds

2 tablespoons fennel seeds

1 tablespoon black peppercorns

4 large lamb shanks (1 to 1½ pounds each)

Kosher salt and freshly ground black pepper

Extra-virgin olive oil

1 large white onion, cut into 1½-inch pieces

3 celery stalks, cut crosswise into 1½-inch lengths

2 carrots, peeled and cut crosswise into 1½-inch lengths

1 small leek, halved, sliced crosswise, and washed well

6 garlic cloves, peeled

3 bay leaves, preferably fresh

1 (16-ounce) can San Marzano tomatoes, with their juices

1 (6-ounce) can tomato paste

3 cups dry red wine

4 cups low-sodium beef broth

4 (12-ounce) bottles Guinness stout

¼ cup chopped fresh thyme leaves

5 fresh marjoram sprigs

1 bunch baby carrots

Juice of 1 lemon

2 bunches watercress, tough stems removed

# Seared Flat-Iron Steak

*with* CREAMED CHARD *and* CARAMELIZED ONIONS

Flat-iron steak is cut from the shoulder but has a texture similar to sirloin, and it has incredible marbling. You might see it labeled "top blade steak" or "patio steak" in different markets. This dish is meaty and fresh all at the same time.

**Bring a large pot** of salted water to a boil. Add the chard to the boiling water and cook for 5 minutes. Drain the chard and, when cool enough to handle, squeeze dry, and coarsely chop.

**Melt 2 tablespoons of** the butter in a large, heavy-bottomed pot over medium heat. Add the diced onions and the garlic and cook slowly until the onions are translucent. Add the cream, fold in the chopped chard, and simmer, reducing the cream mixture until thick, about 15 minutes. Add 1 tablespoon salt, ½ teaspoon pepper, and the grated nutmeg.

**Melt the remaining** 2 tablespoons of butter in a skillet over medium heat. Add the sliced onions and cook until caramel-colored and very soft, 25 to 30 minutes.

**Rub the steak with** olive oil and season liberally with salt and pepper. Heat a large cast iron or other heavy skillet over high heat. Once the pan is hot, add a 2-count of olive oil. Sear the steak without moving for 5 to 8 minutes on one side, then flip, and sear on the second side for another 8 to 10 minutes. Transfer the steak to a cutting board to rest for 10 minutes. While the steak rests, combine the beef broth, lemon juice, and olives in a saucepan. Bring to a boil, reduce the heat, and simmer for 10 minutes.

**To serve, slice the** steak across the grain in ¼-inch-thick slices. Place a scoop of the creamed chard on the bottom of the plate, and top with a few slices of the steak and a few tablespoons of the olive jus. Serve with the grilled bread topped with the caramelized onions.

## Serves 4

2 bunches swiss chard, stems and ribs removed

4 tablespoons (½ stick) unsalted butter

2 yellow onions, sliced, plus ½ yellow onion, finely diced

2 garlic cloves, finely chopped

4 cups heavy cream

Kosher salt and freshly ground black pepper

¼ teaspoon grated nutmeg

2 pounds flat-iron steak

Extra-virgin olive oil

3 cups low-sodium beef broth

Juice of 1 lemon, preferably Meyer lemon

½ cup good-quality pitted mixed olives

4 (½-inch-thick) baguette slices, grilled

# The Ultimate Beef Wellington

*with* MUSHROOM GRAVY

Like Baked Alaska, Beef Wellington is old-school restaurant fare that deserves a second look. It's not nearly as hard to make as it seems, and you can't help but think *special occasion* when you see it.

Serves 6 to 8

3-pound center-cut beef tenderloin, trimmed of fat and silver skin

Extra-virgin olive oil

Kosher salt and freshly ground black pepper

1½ pounds white mushrooms

2 shallots, coarsely chopped

1 garlic clove, coarsely chopped

2 tablespoons unsalted butter

3 tablespoons fresh thyme leaves

12 thin slices prosciutto

2 tablespoons Dijon mustard

All-purpose flour, for rolling

1 pound frozen puff pastry, thawed

1 large egg, lightly beaten

Mushroom Gravy (page 246)

**Tie the tenderloin with** kitchen string in four places so that it holds its cylindrical shape while cooking. Rub it all over with olive oil, then season it liberally with salt and pepper. Heat a large, heavy skillet over high heat and when hot add the beef and sear on all sides, including the ends, until well browned. Don't skimp on this, it's an important flavor-building step. Set the meat aside on a platter to cool.

**Combine the mushrooms,** shallots, and garlic in a food processor. Pulse until finely chopped. Add the butter and 2 tablespoons of olive oil to the pan you seared the beef in and heat over medium heat. Add the chopped mushroom mixture and 1 tablespoon of the thyme and sauté for 8 to 10 minutes, until most of the liquid has evaporated. Season with salt and pepper and set the duxelles aside to cool.

**Spread a 1½-foot piece** of plastic wrap on your work surface and arrange the prosciutto on top, overlapping the slices in a rectangle large enough to wrap around the beef tenderloin. Use a rubber spatula to cover the prosciutto evenly with a thin layer of the mushroom duxelles. Sprinkle the duxelles with salt, pepper, and the remaining 2 tablespoons thyme leaves. Remove the twine from the beef and smear it lightly all over with the mustard. Center the beef on the duxelles, then use the wrap to bring the prosciutto up and around the beef, tucking in the ends of the prosciutto as you roll. Twist the ends of the plastic and refrigerate the roll for 30 minutes.

**On a lightly floured** surface, roll the puff pastry out to about a ¼-inch thickness. (Depending on the size of your sheets you may have to overlap 2 sheets and press them together to fully enclose the meat.) Remove the

*(continued on page 246)*

plastic from the chilled beef and place the roll in the center of the pastry. Bring the long sides up over the beef, enclosing it completely, brushing the seam with egg wash to seal. Trim the ends if necessary, then brush with egg wash and fold over to completely seal the package. Place the beef seam side down on a greased baking sheet and chill for 1 to 2 hours. Reserve the egg wash, covered, in the refrigerator.

**Preheat the oven to 425ºF.** Brush all of the pastry with the reserved egg wash, then cut a couple of slits in the top to allow the steam to escape as the beef cooks. Roast for 40 to 45 minutes, until the pastry is golden brown and the beef registers 125ºF on an instant-read meat thermometer. Let the beef Wellington rest for 15 to 20 minutes before cutting into thick slices. Serve with the mushroom gravy.

# Mushroom Gravy

**Makes about 4 cups**

1 pound veal bones, cut into small pieces

1 medium carrot, coarsely chopped

1 medium onion, coarsely chopped

2 celery stalks, coarsely chopped

4 garlic cloves, minced

1 tablespoon fresh thyme leaves

Kosher salt and freshly ground black pepper

Extra-virgin olive oil

2 quarts low-sodium beef broth

1 cup red wine

1 bay leaf

2 tablespoons unsalted butter

1 small shallot, finely diced

½ pound white mushrooms, quartered

1 tablespoon all-purpose flour

¼ cup heavy cream

**Preheat the oven to 400ºF.** Combine the bones, carrots, onions, celery, 3 of the garlic cloves, and the thyme in a roasting pan. Season well with salt and pepper and drizzle with olive oil. Roast in the oven for 30 to 40 minutes, until the bones are a deep golden brown. Transfer the pan to the stovetop and add the beef broth, wine, and bay leaf. Bring to a boil, then simmer over medium heat for 25 to 30 minutes. Strain the gravy, discarding the solids, and skim off any fat.

**Heat the butter and** 1 tablespoon extra-virgin olive oil in a skillet over high heat. Add the remaining garlic, the shallots, and the mushrooms, season well with salt and pepper, and cook, stirring, for about 5 minutes, until the mushrooms are golden brown. Dust the mushrooms with the flour. Add 2 cups of the strained veal stock to the pan (freeze the remainder for another use) and stir to smooth out any lumps. Simmer until the flour is cooked and the gravy is thick and rich, about 10 minutes. Stir in the heavy cream. Serve hot.

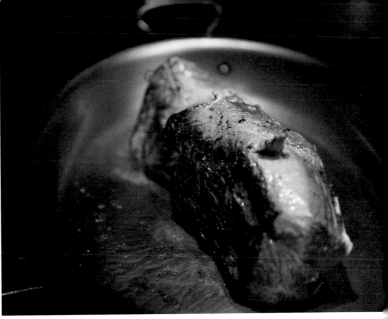

# El Paseo

One of the first neighborhood families Tolan and I became friendly with after moving to Mill Valley is Sammy and Kari Hagar. Most people probably think of Sammy in terms of his music career (Rock and Roll Hall of Fame, anyone?), but what most people don't know is that Sammy has a true love of good food and wine. He never ceases to amaze me with his sophisticated palate and deep connection to the food world. I kid you not, the guy has some of the world's most celebrated chefs on his speed dial. And no, I'm not counting myself.

So I suppose it was a natural thing that he and I would go into business together. We clearly share passions for food, wine, music, and family and we both feel very strongly about the beautiful little town in which we live. While I may be a newbie to this area, Sammy is old-school Mill Valley and when it comes to understanding the culture of a place, that kind of knowledge is invaluable. We knew that there was something to this new-found friendship and after about all of ten seconds, it hit us: Yes, we need to do a restaurant together. And it has to be in Mill Valley. But where?

About a hundred yards from my kitchen shop is a famous old building called "El Paseo," which dates back to 1896. It has operated as a restaurant continuously since 1946, and over the years, it has received some of food and wine's most prestigious honors.

The restaurant, full of original, hundred-year-old brick, is split into four rooms, almost like intimate dining pods, with the signature brick path for which it is named (*el paseo* translates to "the passage" in Spanish) meandering through the middle. As a restaurant, El Paseo holds a very special place in many locals' hearts as it is the grand dame of dining in Mill Valley . . . globally recognized but still locally beloved. There was no question in our minds that our job was to honor the traditions of the space and build upon them.

# Braised Leeks

### *with* TOMATOES *and* SHAVED BOTTARGA

Leeks lend a subtle but very important flavor to my cooking and they are an ingredient I can't do without. Enriched with olive oil and the salty ocean note of bottarga, which is salted, dried mullet or tuna roe, they make my mouth do back flips. God bless the humble leek.

**Serves 4 to 6**

6 large leeks

Extra-virgin olive oil

½ yellow onion, very thinly sliced

4 garlic cloves, very thinly sliced

1 (16-ounce) can San Marzano tomatoes, with their juices

1 teaspoon sugar

2 teaspoons freshly ground black pepper

1 ounce bottarga

1 cup wild arugula

**Begin by removing the** roots of the leeks, as well as the green tops, leaving 1 inch of green intact. Halve lengthwise and rinse really well, making sure to remove all the fine dirt between the layers. Pat dry and set aside.

**Place a medium skillet** over high heat and add a 2-count of oil. Add the onions and garlic and cook, stirring, for 10 minutes, or until the onions are soft. Add the tomatoes and sugar. Reduce the heat to medium and simmer for 30 minutes, stirring now and then. Season with pepper but don't add salt, as the bottarga is very salty.

**Preheat the oven to 375°F.** Arrange the leeks in a single layer in an ovenproof baking dish and cover with the tomato sauce. Bake for 1 hour or until the leeks are soft. Shave the bottarga over the entire dish, and serve topped with the arugula.

# Savoy Cabbage Sauerkraut

*with* GREEN APPLES

Homemade sauerkraut is a meat lover's best friend. When meat juices converge with humble cabbage, plus apples, caraway, and vinegar to balance out the richness, you've got an amazing flavor combination: earthy, comfortable, and truly unforgettable.

**Serves 4 to 6**

3 heads Savoy cabbage

4 tablespoons (½ stick) unsalted butter

1 large yellow onion, halved and sliced

2 green apples, peeled, cored, and sliced

2 tablespoons caraway seeds

1 tablespoon kosher salt

1 teaspoon freshly ground black pepper

4 cups apple cider vinegar

**Begin by pulling off** any of the damaged outside leaves of the cabbage. Slice the cabbage in half the long way and remove the core from the bottom. Thinly slice the cabbage crosswise, into ¼-inch-thick slices. Add the butter to a heavy-bottomed pot and warm over medium-high heat. Once the butter is melted, add the onions and cook until translucent, about 10 minutes. Add the cabbage, apples, caraway seeds, salt, pepper, and vinegar to the pot, cover with a lid, reduce the heat to medium, and cook for 20 minutes, or until the cabbage has cooked but still has a little bite to it. Adjust the final seasoning with salt and pepper.

# Cauliflower Ricotta Pudding

A lighter alternative to mashed potatoes, this bakes up creamy and a bit puffy, with a texture similar to a soft polenta. It makes a fantastic neutral backdrop to rich meat dishes, like the roasted pork shoulder on page 233 or the veal shoulder with porcini mushrooms on page 55.

**Serves 6–8**

4 tablespoons (½ stick) unsalted butter, plus more for greasing the dish

1 head cauliflower, cut into florets

Kosher salt and freshly ground black pepper

1 (16-ounce) container whole-milk ricotta

5 large egg yolks

1 cup grated Parmesan cheese

**Preheat the oven to 325°F.**
Lightly grease a 2-quart baking dish with butter. Bring a pot of salted water to a boil over high heat. Add the cauliflower and blanch until tender, about 5 minutes. Drain the cauliflower and transfer immediately to a food processor. Add the 4 tablespoons butter, season with salt and pepper, and puree until smooth.

Pour the cauliflower puree into a large mixing bowl and whisk in the ricotta, egg yolks, Parmesan cheese, 1 teaspoon salt, and ½ teaspoon pepper. Transfer to the prepared baking dish and bake until the pudding is golden brown and nearly firm in the center, about 50 minutes. Serve warm.

# Roasted Pumpkin

### *with* TOASTED QUINOA, DATES, *and* SAGE

Vegetables are the cornerstone of California cooking, and the seasonal variations of the culinary landscape get me out of bed every day. This pumpkin dish has powerful olfactory associations, evoking a cool autumn night, a warm fire, and cheeks rosy from a glass of amazing pinot noir. Let's see a pork chop do that.

**Serves 8 to 10**

1 small sugar pumpkin (2 to 3 pounds), halved and seeded

Extra-virgin olive oil

Kosher salt and freshly ground black pepper

2 cups quinoa

2 cups pitted and julienned medjool dates

¼ cup small sage leaves

**Preheat the oven to 375°F.** Cut the pumpkin into pieces roughly 3 inches square and arrange on a rimmed baking sheet, skin side down. Drizzle the pumpkin pieces with olive oil and give them a sprinkle of salt and pepper. Roast the pumpkin for 1 hour, or until soft. Once cool enough to handle, peel off and discard the skin, and place the roasted pumpkin flesh in a bowl.

**Place a dry skillet** over medium heat and add the quinoa. Toast for 5 to 10 minutes, or until the quinoa releases a beautiful toasty aroma.

Add 3 cups water and 1 tablespoon kosher salt, cover, and bring to a boil. Reduce the heat to low and simmer the quinoa for 25 minutes, or until all the water has been absorbed. Remove from the heat and set aside, covered; the steam will finish cooking the quinoa.

**Once the quinoa** has cooled off a bit, add it to the bowl with the roasted pumpkin along with the dates, torn sage leaves, and ¼ cup of olive oil. Toss gently to combine. Season with more salt and pepper. Serve at room temperature.

# Paradise Valley

Up Highway 1 from Mill Valley, along the coast, is the farm community of Bolinas. It's only about twenty-five miles from where I live, but it is truly worlds away. There, Paradise Valley Produce is run by two amazing farmers, Dennis and Sandy Dierks, who've lived virtually off the grid for about thirty-five years. The farm has been certified organic since 1972 and represents an era of farming that is wholly unique and, from a chef's perspective, completely amazing. As I worked on the menu for El Paseo, I asked Dennis and Sandy if I could visit them to learn more about how their local farm could play a part in our restaurant. It's one thing to buy local produce and yet another to

actually walk the fields and hand-harvest amazing produce. Dennis, Sandy, and I walked through rows of gorgeous rainbow chard, multiple varieties of hearty kale, fragrant green garlic, and delicate pea tendrils. To hear their personal story of maintaining a small family-run farm in a world of mega-market expansion and simultaneously experience the bounty of their years of dedication was truly inspiring. Just a few yards from the fields—where my dog, Jake, and his new farm-dog buddies chased off deer and hawks—Dennis got the communal fire pit going and we got to cooking up the day's bounty. As we worked with their beautiful produce, I couldn't help but feel the embrace of their sense of pride and place. Paradise Valley is enchanting and produces delicious food, and if you ever have the chance to visit a farm, I think it'll change the way you think about your food.

# Roasted California Fennel

*with* OLIVE TAPENADE, FETA, *and* MINT

There's a reason visitors to northern California are inevitably reminded of Italy or France: They not only share world-class winemaking, but they also share many similar culinary ingredients. In the summer, the air in northern California is alive with wild rosemary, laurel, and—the hero in this recipe—fresh fennel. Slow-roasting fennel caramelizes its natural sugars and softens what in a raw state is a very crisp texture to a texture something like that of a rich roasted onion. Serve it with lamb, chicken, and pork.

**Serves 4 to 6**

4 fennel bulbs with tops

Extra-virgin olive oil

Kosher salt and freshly ground black pepper

2 cups pitted green olives

3 small garlic cloves, peeled

1 teaspoon dried red pepper flakes

¼ cup chopped fresh flat-leaf parsley

¼ cup chopped fresh tarragon

2 tablespoons chopped drained capers

1 tablespoon red wine vinegar

3 ounces feta cheese. crumbled

1 cup torn fresh mint leaves

**Preheat the oven to 375°F.** Discard the fennel stalks, reserving the fronds for garnish. Halve the bulbs lengthwise and rub with olive oil, salt, and pepper. Place cut side down in a roasting pan and roast until soft and caramelized, about 1 hour and 15 minutes.

**To make the olive** tapenade combine the green olives, garlic, red pepper flakes, parsley, tarragon, capers, vinegar, and 3 tablespoons of olive oil in a food processor and pulse until chunky.

**To serve, arrange the** roasted fennel on a big platter. Drizzle with the tapenade, then sprinkle the feta cheese, mint leaves, and fennel fronds over all.

# Wayfare Tavern Popovers

When it comes to classic American breads, no one denies that aristocratic British Yorkshire pudding begat the humble popover; the difference is that popovers are better, more of a buttery balloon than a fat-soaked egg pudding. Popovers first appeared in American literature as far back as the 1850s, and to this day I've yet to meet anyone who didn't love them.

**Makes 12 popovers**

6 large eggs, at room temperature

3½ cups whole milk, at room temperature

4 tablespoons (½ stick) unsalted butter, melted and cooled

4 cups bread flour

1½ teaspoons kosher salt

1 teaspoon baking powder

**In a blender, combine** the eggs, milk, and melted butter. Blend on high until smooth, about 10 minutes. In a large bowl, sift together the bread flour, salt, and baking powder. Add the dry mixture to the wet and blend, scraping down the sides as necessary, until just combined, 10 to 15 seconds. Place the top on the blender and let the batter sit, at room temperature, for 1 hour.

**Preheat the oven to 450°F.** Place an oven rack in the middle position and place an empty popover pan on the rack. Once the pan is hot, remove it and coat evenly with nonstick spray. Working quickly, fill the molds almost to the top with batter. Immediately place back in the oven and bake for 15 minutes, then reduce the heat to 375°F and bake for an additional 20 to 25 minutes, or until the popovers are a deep golden brown color. It is very important to not open the door as the popovers bake, as it could cause them to collapse. Once they are golden brown, remove from the baking pan and let cool on a wire rack. With a skewer, carefully pierce the sides of the popovers to allow the steam to escape. This will keep the popovers crispier for longer.

# Shoestring French Fries

## FRIED *in* DUCK FAT

Since we're going there, let's go all the way. If you don't happen to have any clarified duck fat around the house, you can find it at Whole Foods, and you won't regret it. I like fries cut thin, so that when they're fried crisp they add crunch to your plate while soaking up all the juices. And it's not like you're eating a whole basket of these tasty little guys, right? Right?

**Serves 6**

3 pounds russet potatoes

3 quarts pure duck fat

6 garlic cloves, unpeeled and smashed with the side of a chef's knife

2 fresh rosemary sprigs

Kosher salt and freshly ground black pepper

**Peel and cut the** potatoes on a mandoline or food processor fitted with the julienne blade. Soak the potatoes in cold water for 20 minutes, then drain. Replace the water and soak for 30 minutes longer. This will rinse away much of the starch, making a better French fry. Drain the potatoes well and blot as dry as possible.

**Heat the duck fat to 365°F** in a large, heavy-bottomed pot, taking care to fill the pot no more than halfway for safety.

**Once the fat has** reached 365°F, dip the end of one piece of potato into the fat; if it bubbles immediately, the fat is ready. Drop the whole garlic cloves and rosemary sprigs into the fat. This will release all their wonderful flavors, seasoning not only the fat, but the French fries, too.

**Add the potatoes in** small batches, so that the fat's temperature doesn't drop too much. Fry until the potatoes are golden brown and crispy, 6 to 8 minutes per batch, then remove with a slotted spoon to paper towels to drain. Season immediately with salt and pepper. Repeat with the remaining potatoes. Before serving, scoop out the fried garlic and rosemary and toss with the fries.

# Sweet Endings

# Butterscotch Pudding

Desserts like butterscotch pudding totally fit the vibe of the Wayfare Tavern menu. It's creamy and authentically American, and, when it's done right, it tastes amazing. Right after this photo was shot, I devoured the bowl in about four bites. If you look hard, you can see me in the reflection of the glass, drooling.

**Serves 4 to 6**

4 tablespoons (½ stick) unsalted butter

1 vanilla bean, split

1 cup packed dark brown sugar

3 tablespoons cornstarch

2½ cups whole milk

2 large eggs

1 teaspoon kosher salt

1 tablespoon Scotch whiskey

Fresh whipped cream, for garnish

Toffee chips, for garnish

**Melt the butter in** a large saucepan over low heat. Scrape the seeds from the vanilla bean into the pan and then add the bean and the brown sugar. Simmer gently just until the sugar dissolves, then remove from the heat.

**In a small bowl,** whisk together the cornstarch with ½ cup of the milk until smooth. Then whisk in the eggs.

**Slowly pour the remaining** 2 cups of milk into the melted brown sugar mixture while whisking constantly. Once this is smooth, whisk in the egg mixture. Return the pan to the stove and, whisking constantly, bring to a simmer over medium-high heat. Once the mixture begins to bubble, reduce the heat to low and continue to cook for 1 to 2 minutes, remembering to constantly whisk. Once the mixture thickens and reaches the texture of hot fudge, remove it from the heat. Stir in the salt and the Scotch. Pour the pudding into 4 to 6 serving glasses, and cover with plastic wrap, making sure to press it directly on top of the pudding. Serve with fresh whipped cream and toffee chips.

# Caramelized Pears

*with* RUM-RAISIN MASCARPONE

A good family friend is a health nut who also suffers from celiac disease, for which he follows a gluten-free diet. I created this dessert especially for him and it was simple, yet flavorful and memorable. I didn't sprinkle the amaretti cookies on top of his pear, of course, but he didn't seem to miss them as he licked his plate clean.

**Serves 8**

*Rum-Raisin Mascarpone*

8 ounces mascarpone cheese

½ cup light rum

½ cup granulated sugar

1½ teaspoon fresh lemon juice

½ cup tightly packed golden raisins, soaked in ¼ cup warm water for 30 minutes

---

4 Bosc pears

¼ cup packed light brown sugar

3 tablespoons unsalted butter

½ teaspoon fresh lemon juice

4 amaretti cookies, crushed

**Make the rum-raisin**
mascarpone: In a medium bowl, whisk the mascarpone cream gently to loosen it up. Whisk in the rum, granulated sugar, and lemon juice. Drain the raisins and stir into the cream.

**Preheat the oven to 375°F.**

**Halve the unpeeled pears**
lengthwise and use a melon-baller or teaspoon to scoop out the cores. Combine the brown sugar and butter in a large ovenproof skillet over medium-high heat and stir until just melted. Add the lemon juice then place the pears in the skillet, cut side down. Baste the pears with the melted butter and sugar. Slide the skillet into the oven and roast the pears for 15 to 17 minutes until the pears are tender. Baste the pears once more and set aside to cool in their cooking liquid.

**Serve the pears topped** with a scoop of mascarpone cream and drizzle with the pan juices. Top with amaretti crumbs.

# Pear and Walnut Pie

### *with* APPLE BUTTER CRÈME FRAÎCHE

Listen, I admire the beautiful, deconstructed fantasy desserts you can get in most "nice" restaurants these days, but I can rarely remember them the next day–they don't really speak to me on an emotional level. Let's hear it for a good old-fashioned American pie.

**Make the pie dough:** Fill a 1-cup measuring cup with water and add a few ice cubes. In a large bowl, whisk together the flour, granulated sugar, and salt. Sprinkle the butter cubes over the flour and use a pastry blender or 2 knives to cut the butter into the flour. When the butter pieces are the size of tiny peas, you're done; do not overmix.

**Drizzle ¹/₂ cup of** the ice water over the butter and flour mixture and use a rubber or silicone spatula to mix the dough, adding more cold water a tablespoon at a time as needed to bring it together. Once you're pulling large clumps with the spatula, use your hands to finish mixing, gathering the damp clumps together into one mound and giving the mass a few quick kneads.

**Divide the dough in half** and wrap each portion in plastic, using the sides to shape the dough into a disk. Let the dough chill in the fridge for at least 1 hour before rolling.

**Preheat the oven to 350°F.**
Spread the walnuts on a rimmed baking sheet and toast until they are golden brown, about 10 minutes, stirring once or twice. Let the nuts cool for a few minutes, then coarsely chop. Leave the oven on.

**Peel and core the** pears and cut into ¹/₈-inch slices. Place the pears and walnuts in a large mixing bowl and add the brown sugar, honey, flour, cinnamon, rum, lemon juice, and salt. Toss gently to combine thoroughly.

**Lightly flour a work** surface and roll out 1 dough disk to a slightly larger diameter than a 9-inch pie pan. Lay the dough in the pan and fill with the pear and walnut mixture. Roll out

*(continued on page 276)*

**Makes one 9-inch pie**

### *Flaky Pie Dough*

2½ cups all-purpose flour, plus more for rolling

1 tablespoon granulated sugar

1 teaspoon kosher salt

1 cup (2 sticks) very cold unsalted butter, cut into ½-inch cubes

---

½ cup walnuts

8 Bosc pears

1 cup lightly packed light brown sugar

2 tablespoons honey

1 tablespoon all-purpose flour

2 teaspoons ground cinnamon

2 tablespoons dark rum

2 tablespoons fresh lemon juice

½ teaspoon kosher salt

1 egg, lightly beaten

8 ounces crème fraîche

½ cup apple butter

the remaining dough and place over the filling. Trim the excess dough to a 1-inch overhang and use your fingers to crimp the edges. Brush the crust with the egg wash. Cut a round hole in the center of the pie and make several 1-inch slits in the crust. Place the pie tin on a baking sheet to catch any drips.

**Bake the pie for** 40 to 50 minutes, or until the crust is a beautiful golden brown. Let the pie cool for at least 15 minutes before serving warm or at room temperature.

**Whip the crème fraîche** until fluffy. Add the apple butter and stir until somewhat incorporated; you should be able to see swirls of the apple butter.

**Serve the pie with** dollops of crème fraîche.

# Apple Dumplings

## with CINNAMON SABAYON *and* SALTED CARAMEL SAUCE

While some apple dumplings are enclosed in a pastry crust, these have a golden crumb coating that makes them significantly lighter and more delicate. You'll want to serve the salted caramel sauce with every dessert you can think of.

**Combine the cider,** cinnamon sticks, and star anise in a deep saucepan and bring almost to a boil. Drop in the whole, unpeeled apples and cover with a piece of parchment paper. Cook gently over low heat for 15 minutes, or just until the apples are beginning to feel soft. Remove from the heat.

**Preheat the oven to** 375ºF. In a mixing bowl, stir together the breadcrumbs, brown sugar, melted butter, and cinnamon. Pour the buttermilk into a deep bowl. One at a time, dip the poached apples into the buttermilk, then roll them in the bread-crumb mixture. Place the coated apples on a baking sheet and bake for 30 to 40 minutes, or until the apples are soft all the way through and the bread crumbs are golden brown.

**To make the caramel sauce:** Combine the sugar, corn syrup, and ¼ cup of water in a medium saucepan, and bring to a boil. Cook over high heat until the caramel is a deep amber color, about 6 minutes. Remove the saucepan from the heat and carefully whisk in the cream, butter, and salt, stirring until smooth. Keep warm.

**To make the sabayon:** Bring 2 inches of water to a simmer over medium heat in a medium saucepan. In a metal bowl, combine the egg yolks, prosecco, sugar, cinnamon, and 2 tablespoons of the cider poaching liquid. Place the bowl over the simmering water and whisk constantly until the liquid has doubled in volume and is very light, thick, and frothy, 5 to 7 minutes.

**To serve:** Spoon a few tablespoons of the caramel on each plate and place an apple on top. Spoon a few tablespoons of the sabayon over each apple.

### Serves 4

1 quart unfiltered apple cider

2 cinnamon sticks

2 star anise

4 pink lady apples

3 cups panko breadcrumbs

½ cup light brown sugar, packed

2 tablespoons melted butter

1 teaspoon ground cinnamon

2 cups buttermilk

### Salted Caramel Sauce

1 cup white sugar

2 tablespoons light corn syrup

¾ cup heavy cream

¼ cup (½ stick) unsalted butter

1 teaspoon kosher salt

### Cinnamon Sabayon

6 egg yolks

1 cup prosecco

5 tablespoons sugar

1½ teaspoons ground cinnamon

# Profiteroles

## *with* CHOCOLATE GANACHE

*Profiterole* is a big word for a miniature cream puff. You'll find versions of profiteroles, one of my favorite desserts, on San Francisco menus as far back as 1851, and the European version, filled with anything whipped and light, dates back to the sixteenth century. One version I discovered called for almond broth, cockscomb, and black truffles. I think I'll take mine with vanilla ice cream and chocolate sauce.

**Makes 24 profiteroles; serves 8**

½ cup (1 stick) unsalted butter

1 teaspoon sugar

Pinch of salt

1 cup all-purpose flour

1 teaspoon baking powder

3 large eggs

1 quart vanilla ice cream

Chocolate Ganache (page 282)

Confectioners' sugar, for garnish

**Preheat the oven to 400°F.** Line 2 baking sheets with parchment paper.

**In a heavy-bottomed** saucepan, bring 1 cup water, butter, sugar, and salt to a gentle boil over medium-high heat, stirring with a wooden spoon until the butter is completely melted. Sift the flour and baking powder together, then add all at once and continue to stir until all the flour is incorporated and the dough becomes a mass that pulls away from the sides of the pot. Remove from the heat and scrape the dough into a mixing bowl. Using an electric mixer, beat the dough on medium speed to cool it off a bit. Add the eggs, one at a time, stopping to scrape down the sides of the bowl periodically. When all the eggs have been incorporated, the dough should be a thick, smooth, and glossy paste.

**Scoop the dough into** a pastry bag fitted with a plain round 1-inch tip (or use 2 spoons if you do not have a pastry bag) and pipe 24 golf ball–size mounds onto the prepared baking sheets, allowing 2 inches between them so they can spread as they bake; make the mounds as high and round as possible.

**Bake the cream puffs** for 10 minutes, then reduce the oven temperature to 350°F. and bake for an additional 25 minutes. Do not open the oven door or remove the

*(continued on page 282)*

pans from the oven until the cream puffs are golden brown and well risen. Transfer to a cooling rack and cool completely.

**Using a serrated knife,** slice off the top two-fifths of each cream puff. Fill each profiterole with a small scoop of ice cream and replace the top. Place 3 profiteroles on each plate, drizzle with the chocolate ganache, and sprinkle with confectioners' sugar.

# Chocolate Ganache

### Makes 2 cups

¾ cup heavy cream

1 tablespoon unsalted butter

½ pound semisweet chocolate, cut into chunks

¼ teaspoon pure vanilla extract

**Combine the cream and** butter in a small heavy-bottomed saucepan over medium heat. Heat the mixture until bubbles appear around the sides of the pan, but do not allow the cream to boil. Stir in the chocolate and vanilla and remove from the heat. Stir the ganache until the chocolate melts and the sauce is smooth.

# Baked Alaska

This amazing American dessert rarely shows up on menus unless you're dining on a cruise ship. The ice cream base uses the bowl of a stand mixer as a mold, giving you a proper Mount McKinley to work with. Add a topping of toasted meringue and a flaming Grand Marnier sauce poured tableside and you have a dessert that people won't soon forget. This is a great reason to bust out that butane kitchen torch you bought to make crème brûlée; just skip the broiling step.

**Serves 10 to 12**

2 cups all-purpose flour

1½ cups sugar

1 tablespoon baking powder

½ teaspoon kosher salt

8 large eggs, separated

½ cup fresh orange juice

½ cup vegetable oil

1 tablespoon pure vanilla extract

1 tablespoon grated orange zest

2 teaspoons grated lemon zest

½ teaspoon cream of tartar

Chocolate ice cream, softened

Swiss Meringue (page 285)

**Preheat the oven to 325°F.** In a large mixing bowl, sift together the flour, sugar, baking powder, and salt. In the bowl of a stand mixer, beat the egg yolks until thick and fluffy, about 3 minutes. Beat in the orange juice, oil, ¼ cup water, the vanilla, orange zest, and lemon zest. Make a well in the flour mixture and pour in the orange mixture, beating until smooth, about 5 minutes. In a clean bowl, beat the egg whites on high speed until they begin to foam. Add the cream of tartar and beat until the whites form stiff peaks. Gently fold the egg whites into the batter.

**Pour the batter into** an ungreased 13 by 18-inch rimmed baking sheet, smooth the top, and bake for 25 to 30 minutes, or until the cake springs back when touched. Let cool completely in the pan.

**Find a domed metal** bowl with an 8-inch diameter or use a spare bowl from your stand mixer. Pack the softened ice cream into the bowl (if you're using the mixer bowl it won't be completely full), making sure to press it in firmly to avoid air pockets. Place the bowl in the freezer to refreeze the ice cream.

**To assemble the baked** Alaska, place a round cake pan or plate about 1 inch larger in diameter than the ice cream bowl on top of the sheet cake and carefully cut around it with a knife (save the scraps for snacks or lunch boxes). Place the

*(continued on page 285)*

cake round on a plate. Dampen a clean kitchen towel and heat it in the microwave for 30 seconds. Remove the bowl of ice cream from the freezer and wrap the towel around the bowl for a minute to loosen the ice cream. Quickly invert the ice cream dome onto the cake round. The ice cream dome should be centered on the cake. Place the baked Alaska in the freezer for 10 minutes to firm the ice cream again.

**Preheat the oven to 500°F** while you make the Swiss meringue. (If you have a kitchen torch you can skip the preheating.)

**Transfer the Swiss meringue** to a pastry bag fitted with a 1-inch plain round tip. Quickly dot the entire cake with meringue spikes, covering the ice cream completely. (If you don't have a pastry bag, simply use a spatula to cover the entire cake. Although it will not have the same dramatic effect, it will taste just as good.) Slide the cake into the oven to brown the meringue, about 6 to 8 minutes, or brown the meringue with a kitchen torch. Serve immediately.

# Swiss Meringue

10 egg whites

2 ¼ cups sugar

½ teaspoon cream of tartar

**Place the egg whites** and sugar in a stainless steel bowl or the top of a double boiler. Place over simmering water and whisk continuously until the mixture is warm (about 120°F). Transfer the mixture to the bowl of a stand mixer and beat on high speed until peaks form and the meringue is completely cooled, 10 to 15 minutes.

# Acknowledgments

So many people helped bring this book together:

Photographer John Lee, thank you for your vision, patience, humor, and stellar talent.

Alison Attenborough, Dorothy's "Godmother of Style." We love her for her class, organization, leadership, and amazing food styling.

My editor, Pam Krauss. Where do I start? You have taught me so much throughout the years and give me nothing but the best guidance and advice. My books are better because of you. Thank you.

Ruba Abu-Nimah, my designer and collaborator. You design a mean book, not to mention all of the other things you've done for us—the wine labels, our retail logos, and more. You have a true gift, and we love working with you and Eleanor Rogers.

John Mucci, Diane Melkonian, and Rick Eisenberg. I am forever indebted to you for holding down the fort on a daily basis and keeping the entire Florence Group team together.

My father, Winston Florence, flew out and stayed with us for the entire book shoot. He made everyone lunch and took care of the gang and Grand-mommy, too!

My wife, Tolan. You keep everything together for me personally and professionally. Most important, you give me a wonderful family to come home to every night; you fill our garage with interesting dishes, props, napkins, and serving dishes, each one thoughtfully selected with love—all while being a fabulous mother to our children, Miles, Hayden, and Dorothy, and to Jake and our 3,000 baby honeybees.

We purchased all of the groceries for this book from our favorite local grocery store, the Mill Valley Market. Thank you to the Canepa Family and the entire team for your help, deliveries, and amazing local ingredients. A special thank-you to our family at the Tyler Florence Shops: Tamara, JJ, Kathe, Charlie, Kelly, Sarah, Daniel, Billy, Kristen, and Joy.

One of my favorite days during the book shoot was the neighborhood family potluck day. Thank you to all of our friends and family who participated and shared their family recipes for the book, especially Candy DeBartolo, whose famous coconut cake is finally getting the recognition it deserves.

I have great business partners. Rick and Anne Ronald let us shoot in their beautiful home, and the Hagar Family came and shot the cover with us on the patio at El Paseo. I am really fortunate to work with partners that I also consider friends: Mike and Kristen House, Lori and Paul Yeomans, Max and Jillian MacKenzie, the Tolucay Team, the Outset Team, Christopher Peacock and Lane Brooks, the Food Network, and the Mondavi Family.

Shooting a book in our home is no walk in the park. It's filled with kids, dogs, honeybees, and a lot of silly rules. Extreme quiet during nap times, no knives on the counters when the kids are in the kitchen, no parking outside of the white lines or the kooky neighbor calls the police, etc. Every-one who worked on the book deserves a special shoutout: Liz Antle, Jamie Prouten, Alana Robinson, Courtney Dougherty, Lala, Poppy, Anthony Hoy Fong, Kevin Crafts, Michael Coleman, Ron Collings, Aaron Sampson, Jim Cardosa, Black Point Sports Club, the Dierks Family, Granny, Gramp, Big Papa and Grandmommy, Janet and Chuck, Robert Price, Olivia Baniuszewicz and Yelena Nesbit at Rodale, and Andrew Freeman and Company for handling our PR.

And, of course, there would be nothing in this book without our creative friends and contributors: Heath Ceramics, Bill and Nicolette Niman, Juliska, Paradise Valley Farms, Far West Funghi, Cowgirl Creamery, Cayson Designs, Boccalone (Chris and Tatiana Cosentino), the Wooden Duck, McEvoy Olive Oil, Preferred Meats Inc., ABS Seafood Company, Prather Ranch Meats, the Smoked Olive, and Golden Gate Meat Company.

Last but not least, thank you to my family and Jake Bacon Florence. I love you all.

# Index

# D

# E

# F

# G

# H

# I

# N

# O

# P

# Q

# R

# S

# Conversion Chart

These equivalents have been slightly rounded to make measuring easier.

| VOLUME MEASUREMENTS | | |
| --- | --- | --- |
| U.S. | IMPERIAL | METRIC |
| ¼ tsp | – | 1 ml |
| ½ tsp | – | 2 ml |
| 1 tsp | – | 5 ml |
| 1 Tbsp | – | 15 ml |
| 2 Tbsp (1 oz) | 1 fl oz | 30 ml |
| ¼ cup (2 oz) | 2 fl oz | 60 ml |
| ⅓ cup (3 oz) | 3 fl oz | 80 ml |
| ½ cup (4 oz) | 4 fl oz | 120 ml |
| ⅔ cup (5 oz) | 5 fl oz | 160 ml |
| ¾ cup (6 oz) | 6 fl oz | 180 ml |
| 1 cup (8 oz) | 8 fl oz | 240 ml |

| WEIGHT MEASUREMENTS | |
| --- | --- |
| U.S. | METRIC |
| 1 oz | 30 g |
| 2 oz | 60 g |
| 4 oz (¼ lb) | 115 g |
| 5 oz (⅓ lb) | 145 g |
| 6 oz | 170 g |
| 7 oz | 200 g |
| 8 oz (½ lb) | 230 g |
| 10 oz | 285 g |
| 12 oz (¾ lb) | 340 g |
| 14 oz | 400 g |
| 16 oz (1 lb) | 455 g |
| 2.2 lb | 1 kg |

| LENGTH MEASUREMENTS | |
| --- | --- |
| U.S. | METRIC |
| ¼" | 0.6 cm |
| ½" | 1.25 cm |
| 1" | 2.5 cm |
| 2" | 5 cm |
| 4" | 11 cm |
| 6" | 15 cm |
| 8" | 20 cm |
| 10" | 25 cm |
| 12" (1') | 30 cm |

| PAN SIZES | |
| --- | --- |
| U.S. | METRIC |
| 8" cake pan | 20 × 4 cm sandwich or cake tin |
| 9" cake pan | 23 × 3.5 cm sandwich or cake tin |
| 11" × 7" baking pan | 28 × 18 cm baking tin |
| 13" × 9" baking pan | 32.5 × 23 cm baking tin |
| 15" × 10" baking pan | 38 × 25.5 cm baking tin |
| | (Swiss roll tin) |
| 1½ qt baking dish | 1.5 liter baking dish |
| 2 qt baking dish | 2 liter baking dish |
| 2 qt rectangular baking dish | 30 × 19 cm baking dish |
| 9" pie plate | 22 × 4 or 23 × 4 cm pie plate |
| 7" or 8" springform pan | 18 or 20 cm springform or |
| | loose-bottom cake tin |
| 9" × 5" loaf pan | 23 × 13 cm or 2 lb narrow |
| | loaf tin or pâté tin |

| TEMPERATURES | | |
| --- | --- | --- |
| FAHRENHEIT | CENTIGRADE | GAS |
| 140° | 60° | – |
| 160° | 70° | – |
| 180° | 80° | – |
| 225° | 105° | ¼ |
| 250° | 120° | ½ |
| 275° | 135° | 1 |
| 300° | 150° | 2 |
| 325° | 160° | 3 |
| 350° | 180° | 4 |
| 375° | 190° | 5 |
| 400° | 200° | 6 |
| 425° | 220° | 7 |
| 450° | 230° | 8 |
| 475° | 245° | 9 |
| 500° | 260° | – |